D0102035

running

SERIOUS ABOUT YOUR SPORT

NEWHAM LIBRARIES

90800100039932

About the authors

Running expert **Paul Cowcher** is a personal trainer who has run numerous marathons and trained many others to running success at various distances. A former professional dancer, he has been working in the health and fitness industry for over ten years. He has trained as an advanced instructor (CYO), Pilates mat work (More Fitness) and has many other teaching qualifications in fitness and dance (ISTD).

Tommaso Bernabei is a television and non-fiction writer who graduated from the Metropolitan University of London. His experience in television led him to collaborate with Italian food shows, introducing him into the world of sport nutrition. He is currently the diet planner for an Italian swimming club and writing a book of sport nutrition recipes.

Sports psychologist **Russell Murphy** runs Personalmindtrainer (www.personalmindtrainer.com) and works regularly with different sportspeople, including advising marathon runners, golfers, duathletes, triathletes and footballers among others. A member of the World Federation of Hypnotherapists, he also gives talks on motivation to major corporations and runs smoking cessation, weight management, confidence, phobias and other treatment programmes.

Photo Credits

Thanks to Runners Need (www.runnersneed.co.uk) for information on running shoes. Photos: iStock.com and P12. Thad Zajdowicz, www.sxu.hu, Vicky S, www.sxu.hu. P14. 1. Ramasamy Chidambaram, www.sxu.hu. 2. Alex Bramwell, www.istockphoto.com/user_view.php www.sxc.hu. P17. Jocilyn Pope, www.sxc.hu. Pontus Edenberg – www.newsoffuture.com www.sxc.hu. P28. Jonnyberg, www.sxu.hu. P35. Pale, www.sxc.hu. P37. Lusi, www.sxc.hu. P39. Marganz, www.sxc.hu. P44. Mike Bexon for chasemysnail.com. P45. jmolsen, www.sxc.hu. P55. Ariel da Silva Parreira. P82. Jonnyberg, www.sxu.hu. p117. 1. Jonathan Ruchti, Switzerland – www.sxc.hu. 2. Lukas – www.blogonade.de – www.sxc.hu. 3. Jonathan Ruchti, Switzerland, www.sxc.hu. P120. 1 Pedro Simao, www.editae.com.br, www.sxc.hu. 2. Rob Owen-Wahl – www. LockStockPhotography.com, www.sxc.hu. 3. Agata Urbaniak, www.xero.prv.pl, www.sxc.hu. P124. 1. Ove Tøpfer – www.pixelmaster. no, www.sxc.hu. 2. Ove Tøpfer – www.pixelmaster.no, www.sxc.hu. 3. Emre Nacigil, www.atolyekusadasi.com, www.sxc.hu. P128. 1. Anna H-G – www.sxc.hu. 2. Alaa Hamed, users2.titanichost.com/alaasafei, www.sxc.hu. 3. Gunnar Brink, www.sxc.hu. P137. Rob Owen-Wahl, www. LockStockPhotography.com, www.sxc.hu. p136 Kliverap – www.sxc.hu. p136 Brandon Kettle – www.sxc.hu. p136 Johan Bolhuis – www. natuurarts.nl, www.sxc.hu. p137 Pedro Simao – www.editae.com.br, www.sxc.hu. p137 Michael Grunow – www.sxc.hu. p137 Monika M – www.sxc.hu. p138 Gerhard Taatgen jr. – www.taatgen-fotografie.nl, www.sxc.hu. p138 Neil Gould – http://gallery.gouldnet.net, www.sxc.hu. p138 Meekes – www.sxc.hu. p139 Lukas – www.blogonade.de – www.sxc.hu. p139 Matteo Canessa – www.sxc.hu. p139 Chris Greene – www. sxc.hu. p139 Aschaeffer – www.sxc.hu. p140 Brandon W. Mosley – http://www.manjidesigns.com, www.sxc.hu. p140 Steph P – www.sxc. hu. p141 Lavinia Marin – www.sxc.hu. p141 Luca Baroncini – www.cggallery.it, www.sxc.hu. p141 hde2003 – www.sxc.hu. P142-143. Said-w, www. sxc.hu. Notepad graphic. Davide Guglielmo – www.broken-arts.com, www.sxc.hu.

running

SERIOUS ABOUT YOUR SPORT

Paul Cowcher and Tommaso Bernabei

Additional writing by Russell Murphy, Daniel Ford, Remmert Wielinga and Dan Cross

LONDON BOROUGH OF NEWHAM	
90800100039932	
Bertrams	14/10/2011
796.42	£12.99
ANF	NHCT

Contents

Introduction

This book is for you if you run for fun and now want to take your running more seriously. If you have always enjoyed the feel-good factor of running and are thinking of entering a race or you just want to run farther and faster, then this book will give you the knowledge and guidance required to achieve your goals.

This book will help you to train scientifically and get you to the start line in great shape so you can enjoy racing, running and challenging your personal targets.

Many runners start out using running as a form of fitness and a way of keeping their weight down. But once they start enjoying running many people decide to enter races, then the bug has bitten...

The training guidelines included in this book will help you take the next step and you will find your overall fitness levels increase. Having a set target is also a great form of motivation and this can get you out exercising when you would otherwise be tempted to skip a fitness session. It's also advisable to team up with a running partner or two who have similar running speeds or are able to adapt. The other option is to seek out running

clubs; they are probably friendlier and less extremist than you first imagine and great value for money.

Each section in this book is devised to take you through different areas of running fitness. Areas covered include the technical aspects of running, which will help you gain a more economical running style, cross training, stretching and conditioning, and the exercises you will need to do this. The training programmes, covering various times and distances, are provided to help you to gradually build up your running while allowing your body to adapt and strengthen without suffering injury or fitness.

Whatever sport you try, a bit of knowledge can make all the difference in achieving your goals and avoid you getting lost, de-motivated and possibly quitting. The feeling you get when achieving your goals is fantastic, but this does not always happen first time round. As long as your targets are realistic and you keep plugging away you will get there eventually (and have a lot of fun along the way).

Many runners also discover a community and social network they never realized existed. Even if it's just a nod from a runner you see on your regular route, it is always

inspiring to see others getting out there and getting on with it.

There are many people around who seem to put running down, trying to give it a bad name by saying it is bad for you and running long distances will mean you won't be able to walk when you are older. While there is a risk of injury in running, or indeed any sport you do regularly, if you follow the guidelines provided in this book then there is every reason to believe you will suffer only a few muscle aches from a good, hard, enjoyable run.

Running has brought pleasure to many lives with many people progressing from the occasional jog to completing races from 10 km to marathons. The endless hours out on the roads or across fields bring a great feeling of freedom and a time to enjoy your own space. Enjoy your training and keep at it – you will then achieve your goals and keep improving. The aim of this book is for you to learn how to train more scientifically and to feel the same passion that thousands of runners around the world feel every day come wind, rain or shine.

the basics

// GETTING STARTED
// TRAINING PRINCIPLES
// SLEEP, FOOD, FLUID

Getting started

So you have been running for a while and enjoying it and now you have decided you want to start to get serious about your training. But where do start? First, you have to ask yourself if you are physically fit enough to step up and put in some serious training or whether you should stay as a casual runner.

Before embarking on any training programme you should always check with your doctor to make sure you are physically fit for the challenge – especially if you have any doubts about your health or any niggling injuries.

Next you have to decide if you have enough time on your hands to commit to a training programme that dedicates more time to your running. Do you have the time to get serious about your sport?

You also have to consider work and family commitments and put every-thing into balance. It's certainly not

impossible to have young children, a demanding job and still train hard out on the road but it will require a lot of planning and determination.

Once you have decided to go for it you next have to define your goals. What are you training for and why? Do you just want to extend the distance you can run or are you looking for faster, sharper speed?

Of course, for many of you it will be a competitive race that is on your agenda. If that is the case then you need to decide which distance is right for you and set yourself a time target for the race.

It doesn't matter if your aims are to be a champion runner or if you are content competing against yourself, by making sure you get into the right shape you will make the training far more effective and enjoyable. Don't expect to achieve everything overnight: you need to choose realistic goals and have

a realistic time scale for when you want to reach the goals. Start by writing down what you want out of your training and what your goals are; this will help you visualize where you are going and help to keep you focused as your training gets more intense.

When you have developed a long-term plan you will be more able to decide what type of training is best for you and how you can get the most out of your training programme. You may have a target competition you want to train for or you might simply want to run a 10 km or a marathon in a new personal best time.

By setting targets and goals you can focus on what you want to achieve and help keep motivation levels high while you are training. Good luck! Training can be hard work and at times lonely, but the rewards can be huge. Don't be deterred, just keep your eye on the end results.

The principles of training

The **SPORT** principles of training are aimed at helping you understand the training process and allowing you to plan your training so you see a steady upward progression in results.

Specificity – making sure your training is specific to what you are hoping to achieve. Simply put, don't spend all your time doing sprint training sets if you want to improve your long-distance running!

Progression – the body adapts to increased training loads and this will result in improved fitness levels and competitive performance.

Overload – training at a level that will push you. If you are always training at the same intensity and at the same speed you will not see the progression you would hope for. You need to be constantly overloading your muscles and cardio respiratory system to improve your strength and fitness level.

Reversibility – if you don't train or you decrease your intensity then you will see your fitness levels drop and as a consequence so will your overall performance. If you are unwell and are unable to train for an extended period then you will notice a reduced performance level when you start training again.

Tedium – keeping the training interesting. If you find yourself getting bored then you are less likely to want to train and your motivation levels will automatically drop, which can lead to a reduced effort level and even the likelihood of skipping training sessions. This will lead to Reversibility occurring.

When you start to plan your training programme you can use the FITT principles to work towards SPORT. For instance, to make sure that the SPORT principles of Progression and Overload are always occurring you can increase the Frequency

of your training sessions, the Intensity of each session or the Time you spend training. To stop Reversibility occurring rapidly you reduce Intensity if feeling sick. To avoid the SPORT principle of Tedium you can change the Type of training methods you are using. It is advisable that you only change one aspect of the training at a time rather than changing everything otherwise it can be too much for your body and may lead to an injury occurring.

Frequency – how often you train.

Intensity – intensity you train at.

Time – how long you train for.

Type – which training methods you are using.

Sleep, food and fluid

Getting your work-to-rest ratio right is crucial, as an imbalance will lead to over-training, which may result in a decreased performance in training and racing, as well as an increased chance of injury. Put simply: rest is as important as the training itself. As you get fitter you will be able to train longer as long as you keep getting quality rest.

- Set a schedule: be strict in your sleep regime. Sleep and wake at the same time every day including weekends and try to get at least eight hours of rest. Disrupting this schedule may lead to insomnia. 'Catching up' by sleeping extra on weekends makes it harder to wake up early on Monday morning because it re-sets your sleep cycles.

- Exercise: daily exercise will help you sleep, although a workout too close to your bedtime may disrupt your sleep. For maximum benefit try to get your exercise about five to six hours before going to bed.

- Avoid caffeine, nicotine, and alcohol. Don't take these stimulants close to your bedtime. Remember there is caffeine in coffee, chocolate, soft drinks, non-herbal teas, diet drugs and some pain relievers. Don't smoke a cigarette before going to bed as nicotine goes straight to the sleep centres of your brain and will result in a bad night's rest. Alcohol can decrease the time required to fall asleep. However, too much alcohol consumed within an hour of bedtime will deprive you of deep sleep and REM sleep (the sleep that rejuvenates your body the best) and it will keep you in the lighter stages of sleep.

- Relax before bed: reading, listening to music, having sex, taking a warm bath, can all make it easier to fall asleep. You can train yourself to associate certain activities with sleep and make them part of your bedtime ritual. If you can't get to sleep, don't just lie in bed – relax and do something else (like the previously mentioned activities) until you feel tired.

- Control your room temperature: make sure that you sleep in a room that is cool – 18-19 °C (64-66 °F) with 65 per cent of humidity is ideal – as well as dark and quiet.

So train hard and rest well. Nutrition can help supplement your training by giving you the right balance of energy to train and the proteins, vitamins and minerals to help you recover. If you are not getting the right levels of carbohydrates, proteins, fats and vitamins you will quickly feel tired in training and will fail to recover properly, which can lead to fatigue and maybe illness and injury. Hydration is critical, as the body has to be topped up to perform at its peak. Even a one per cent drop in hydration levels will impair your performance. Get used to taking on fluids.

From a busy lifestyle to race day

A busy lifestyle

It's pretty simple: if you do not train consistently you will not see the improvements or get the results you want in your running. The biggest obstacle you can face in getting consistent runs under your belt is a busy lifestyle. But it's not impossible to go from thinking you don't have time to even breathe to training hard, entering a race and, who knows, even hitting the infamous 'wall' yourself one day.

In general most people have to fit their runs in around family and work. This is where you have to be creative. Many runners get their long Sunday runs out of the way before anyone else is up so not to impact on their family life. Even if you do run early, as long as you eat properly after training you will feel great for the rest of the day. Other tips are to run into work, or if you live too far for that then get off the bus or train en route to work and run in the rest of the way. If you pick your children up from school, try to go early so you can run near to where you are picking them up. If you take them to after-school clubs take your running shoes with you. Get your training days established with gentle jogs before you start the running programme. You will soon discover there *is* time to run.

Race-day preparations

In simple terms be organized. Have your running kit and everything else you need prepared the day before. Know what is provided at the race and what you will have to take (you will need pre- and post-drinks and food, and for the long races a comfy pair of shoes to put on after the race). Have all this in your running bag so there are no late panics.

If you are racing away from home and need any accommodation make sure it is pre-booked and you know the logistics of how you are getting to the race line, where you leave your running bag, where you are collecting your bags from, and how you are getting back. The big events are incredibly well organized but if you have 30,000 runners heading towards one start line, there will always be some problems getting there. Allow plenty of time to get to the start as you do not want to be stressed before a race and use up valuable energy.

For the half- and full marathons a warm-up will not be necessary as you should start slowly and build your pace gradually. For 10 km runs you will need a good 15 minutes warm-up, building up to race pace for the last few strides. Add a gentle pre-stretch and then you will be ready for the off.

Hitting the wall

When you were worried about your busy lifestyle, you never thought this would be a problem did you? In reality the wall should only be a problem in the marathon. In simple terms, hitting the wall happens when your glycogen levels (carbohydrates once they have been converted) start running out. Glycogen is your main source of energy when running endurance events and once this is depleted your body will revert to using fat stores as energy, which can leave you feeling very flat and unable to perform at the same intensity. This typically happens at about the 30 km (about 19 mile) mark because a body can only store approximately 2,000 kcal of glycogen, which runs out at about this distance.

You can get your glycogen levels up with sports drinks and gels. The general rule of thumb is to take a sports drink before the race and a gel every 6 km (about 4 miles) or so. However you must try this in training (your long runs are an ideal time to practice) and carefully follow the instructions on the gel pack. They all vary on frequency of use, some have caffeine in, which may not agree with you, and you will need to drink water soon after consumption for most gels.

The other way to prevent your body hitting the wall is through training. By training aerobically for long periods of time your body will adapt and get used to using fat as an energy source earlier. This will then enable you to preserve some of the glycogen stores for longer.

Equipment

When it comes to equipment, running is one of the easiest sports around. After all, people have been running as long as man has existed – all that's needed is a safe, open space and you are away. The finest piece of equipment you'll ever have is your own body so always concentrate on that first and foremost. However, there are a number of items that can enhance your running experience and help improve your training and as you do not need much equipment it will not cost you a fortune to get properly kitted out.

Stopwatch

Although this is a pretty basic tool it is useful in helping you keep track of your running splits and when doing interval training. You do not need to spend a lot of money on this but you will find yourself using it for most runs.

Heart rate monitor

The most important features you will use on a heart rate monitor are those that measure your current heart rate, average heart rate and your highest and lowest heart rates during a run. These are all important for you to measure the intensity of workouts and follow your progress as a runner. The more advanced ones have a lot more features that you can upload to a computer and produce graphs and statistics of your runs. There are some reasonably priced monitors available that will provide you with all the basics.

GPS running watch

This is an optional tool and many elite athletes have successfully trained and competed in races and broken world records without such technology. Having said that, they can be useful and add fun to your running. A GPS watch (many are often just known by their trade name) can also be a great motivational tool and if you are a bit of a statistics freak then there is nothing better than getting home from a long run and checking your kilometre-by-kilometre splits. A watch will show the distance you have run, your speed, gradients you have climbed, as well as averages and other statistics. Once uploaded you can view all this information in graphs. This is a useful tool, as many runners tend to exaggerate or have wishful thinking about the distances they run. A slight word of warning: some runners get almost addicted to the statistics on their watch and can't even run a couple of metres without looking down at it. This will mean you can end up running as fast as you think you should be running, instead of listening to your body and adjusting your speed depending on how your body is responding to the workout that day.

Clothes

Running kit can really vary in price but you do not need to spend a lot of money. All you really need to run is a pair of shorts and a T-shirt, although there are certain situations, such as running in the dark (see The dark on pages 44-45) or the wet (see The wet & other weather conditions on pages 46-47), where you should look at using other clothing. Bright colours (and lights) are crucial for your safety in bad light and there is a lot of dry-fit clothing that works well at drawing the moisture away from the body and keeping some warmth in when it is wet. Running jackets are also useful for the slower training runs on cold days and the high-quality ones are light, comfortable and waterproof (although to a certain extent water always seems to find a way in eventually), allowing an easy running style. They will also normally have some sort of reflector on them to help keep you visible.

Running shoes

Good running shoes are essential. It doesn't matter what they look like, but it is vital they are the correct shoes for you and feel comfortable. You should get your running gait analyzed by an expert so the correct shoes are found for you. It cannot be overestimated how important this is, especially if you are going to be hitting the high-mileage training programmes needed for half- and full marathons. The correct shoes will also help you to avoid injury (see Common running injuries on page 66.) Running shoes are designed for running and are not made for other sports so avoid using them for other activities or they will ruin quickly and need to be replaced.

Running shoes FAQ

I've got a good pair of sports shoes. Can I just run in them or do I need a pair of specialist running shoes?
Running shoes are the single most important piece of kit for anyone taking up running. Running is a high-impact activity and cross trainers, tennis shoes and other athletic shoes do not have enough cushioning to absorb the impact from running. At the same time, running in a pair of old or worn-out running shoes will do more harm than good as cushioning erodes over time. Buying a decent pair of running shoes will protect your joints and reduce the risk of injury.

So what's different about running shoes?
Running shoes are specially designed to provide support and cushion the impact that comes from running. However, not just any running shoe will do and getting the right shoe for you is not as simple as just picking one off the shelf you like the look of or getting a pair a friend has recommended. There is a wide range of running shoes to choose from in a variety of types and styles, with different technology providing varying levels of support and cushioning. Finding the right shoe for you will depend on factors such as your weight, biomechanics and foot shape, along with the surface you run on. That's why it's important to visit a running specialist who will have the expertise to find the right shoe for you. Getting the right shoe can make all the difference to your training, as it will work with your natural biomechanics to boost your running efficiency, maximizing comfort and support and more importantly reducing the risk of injury.

I've heard of pronating and over-pronating. What is that?
Pronation is the inward rolling movement of the foot when it strikes the ground. It helps the body dissipate shock and stabilizes the foot on the ground. Over-pronation is when your foot rolls in excessively during the weight-bearing phase of the gait cycle. There are four main foot types: supinator (or under-pronator), neutral, over-pronator (mild to moderate) and motion control. Most footwear brands produce running shoes that cater for all categories. Depending on your level of over-pronation you will either require a structured cushioned shoe or one with maximum support (motion control). Those who suit the neutral type of shoe are generally bio-mechanically efficient runners who require maximum mid-sole cushioning with minimal arch support. Your pronation pattern is a crucial consideration when it comes to choosing a pair of shoes. Your local running specialist will be able to determine which shoe category you fit into and find the right shoe to suit you.

I'm quite heavy. Do I have to consider anything else when choosing my shoes?
Heavier runners usually require a moderate stability or motion control shoe for support. Steer clear of lightweight performance trainers. Many brands now produce shoes in a varying range of widths so try these out to find which one is right for you.

So how do I go about choosing shoes that fit me?
Visit a running specialist and have your gait analyzed as part of a shoe-fitting assessment. A reputable running store will recommend the most suitable pair of shoes for your running style rather than the most expensive. Along with a wide range of running shoes you'll find staff with the knowledge and expertise to help make the process a little less daunting. The staff should look at your gait and foot strike as you test out different shoes. It can also help to bring along any previous shoes you've been running in as they can reveal a lot about your current style. The staff will often ask about your training goals, running history and surfaces you run on to ensure the shoes match your overall running profile.

Is there any technology that can help me when it comes to choosing shoes?
Many specialist stores offer video gait analysis to determine the most suitable running shoe. This normally involves running on a treadmill

for a short period of time while a camera records your running style. Staff will then take you through the slow motion video replay and explain the biomechanics of your feet by looking at your foot strike and observing foot-and-ankle motion. You should be given the opportunity to try out different shoes to find the most comfortable. Because video gait analysis mimics running it is one of the most accurate methods to determine your foot type.

Do I need a different pair of shoes for training and racing?
Racing flats are lightweight performance trainers and generally not as effective at shock absorption. They have a narrower last and less of a mid-sole than a regular running shoe, which has the advantage of making them more flexible and lightweight. Racing flats are designed to enhance performance in races, particularly over shorter distances or for occasional training use if you're deemed bio-mechanically efficient. Racing flats are generally only recommended for short distances up to half-marathon as they won't provide the same levels of support and cushioning needed to minimize the impact on your body. Average runners are likely to see more benefit from a regular running shoe, which offers the support and cushioning, than a lightweight racer. They are also not suited to heavier runners who need shoes that give adequate support and

comfort. The slower you are the more steps you'll need to take to cover the same distance as a faster runner, thus negating any time-saving benefit anyway. For this reason, racing flats are better suited to faster, efficient runners whose focus is to shave seconds off their time.

How many kilometres should I put into a pair of shoes before using them in a race?
This can vary but you should generally allow about 50-60 kilometres (31-37 miles) or two to three weeks to wear in a running shoe. Start using new shoes for smaller distances and use them in at least one of your longer training runs before using them in a race. It's a good idea to integrate your new pair of shoes while there is still some life left in your current pair so your feet can adjust.

How long do shoes last?
Shoes on average last about 800-950 kilometres (497-590 miles) although this depends on a number of factors including your bodyweight, running style and the surface you run on. Running shoes lose their shock absorption and stability over time and continuing to run in old or worn-out shoes often results in shin and joint pain. The mid-sole of a shoe provides the cushioning and stability and normally wears well before the outsole shows signs of wear and tear. Try squeezing the insole and the outsole at the heel of the shoe

between your thumb and forefinger to check the compression of the mid-sole. Another test is to place both shoes on a flat surface and if the shoes tilt noticeably in or out then that's a good indicator that it's time for a new pair. If you are still in doubt then wear your old shoe on one foot and your new shoe on the other foot. You should notice a remarkable difference.

If I am a really serious runner should I have two pairs and alternate them?
Two pairs is not just for serious runners but you need to be training regularly (most days) or doing high mileage each week before needing two pairs of shoes. Alternating with a second pair will help extend the life of the shoe and prevent uneven wear. However, you will still need to replace each of them after approximately 800-950 kilometres (497-590 miles) so keep a record of when you bought them and a training log.

Do runners of different distances need to look at different things when choosing shoes?
If you mainly sprint or run shorter distances (5 km or less) you may want to look for a lightweight performance shoe which can shave seconds off your performance on race day. If you're undertaking a marathon or undergoing long distance training then you need to ensure the shoe is going to withstand the distance. Look for a shoe designed for high mileage

and perhaps a bit more support than normal because you'll have a tendency to over-pronate more as fatigue sets in. Most importantly, ensure the shoes are a comfortable fit but with plenty of cushioning to ensure a comfortable run. Generally, you'll need a half- to full-size bigger than your regular shoes as the foot expands from time spent on your feet. It's not just the distance that is a deciding factor; you'll also need to consider the surface you run on. If you are regularly training or racing on surfaces other than the road then consider a second shoe designed for that purpose (ie track/distance spike, cross-country spike, trail-running shoe etc).

Are there any other tips that are useful when choosing a pair of shoes?
Preferably shop in the afternoon when your feet will be at their biggest and try shoes on with the pair of socks you'll actually be running in. Try on different pairs of shoes for a comparison – there may be more than one brand that is suitable for you so it will come down to what feels the most comfortable. Don't try to skimp on your running shoes – you may not require the most expensive pair in the shop but you do need decent quality.

When should I use orthotics?
Some runners need specially created insoles (orthotics) to help correct their gait. You may benefit from orthotics in instances where running shoes do not adequately fix your gait when there is a significant discrepancy between your feet or leg length or if you suffer from re-occurring injuries. If this is evident, a reputable running store using video gait analysis should recommend you seek further advice before you buy your running shoes. Generally, corrective orthotics will only require a good, stable neutral shoe. However, this does not apply to everyone and you should get the advice of your podiatrist or orthotist on suggested makes and models. Once you have been fitted for orthotics then bring them along to a specialist store to try out shoes before making a purchase. Ultimately, running shoes and orthotics are designed to work in unison to provide you with the support and cushioning you need – one does not replace the other. Orthotics do take up a bit more room than the manufacturer's shoe liner so you may need a shoe with a deeper heel cup and a wider fit to accommodate them.

technique
& tactics

// SHARPER // SMARTER // MORE EFFICIENT

The basics

This section will help you to improve the way you run and how you approach a race or event. But the best way to improve your running is to get out there and run. You will find your body adapting, running smoother and more efficiently the more you pound out the kilometres.

So why bother assessing how you run? Two reasons: to avoid injury and to run faster with less effort. So, for example, if you find that after running you are experiencing pain in your glutes, there is a chance you are over-striding and you need to make adjustments.

And who is going to complain about running faster for less effort? It is a great feeling when you discover you are covering more distance per stride with less effort. You will start to feel like you are gliding instead of feeling heavy on your feet.

Your body will feel nice and easy when running and your joints will feel easier and happier in their movement. When you wake in the morning you will feel less pain and be ready to train again. When making changes to your technique remember to make them slowly and change only one thing at a time.

Ultimately, though, the best technique is the one that works best for you. Many a good marathon runner has been overtaken by others with terrible technique. Then there are examples of running legends – Paula Radcliffe's head bobbing around, Michael Johnson leaning back as if he were about to fall over – showing that rules are there to be broken.

And many coaches know there are also lots of recreational runners with poor technique who run good progressive times and remain injury free. So work hard at your technique and try whatever you can to improve, but always remember to listen to your body and learn what works for you.

Choosing the correct tactics can also make or break months of training. It is important to look at all the different distances and learn how to pace yourself for them. You also need to know what your goals are. Are you looking to go out there and smash a time, or just win a bet with a friend?

There is a big difference between actually racing and simply aiming for a time target. For many runners the biggest lesson is learning what pace to set to get a great time and aim for a PB. You also need to understand the advantages of running a negative race (faster for the second half) and in the shorter races the importance of getting going right from the off.

It is also crucial to know how to attack hills, mentally and physically. This is an area that can make or break your race. Go too hard up hills and you will expend huge amounts of energy without gaining much time. And gaining confidence running downhill will keep your intensity levels even and help you to gain valuable time.

Improving your technique and tactics can take your running to a higher level. Lessons learnt can give you the tools to run faster, improve your race position and keep you injury free so that your training has as few disruptions as possible. But remember, there is no magic wand. You have to get out there, gradually apply some of the changes you have learnt and get on with it.

Upper body

1 Maintain a tall posture, keeping your shoulders directly above your hips as if there is a straight line drawn between the two pointing directly up.

2 Arms should swing gently backwards and forwards.

3 Keep hands relaxed as if you are holding a piece of paper between your thumb and first finger.

There is no doubt most of the strength work for endurance runners is done in the lower body. Having said that, you will need a strong core to prevent injury, while in the 10 km distance a good arm action can help to propel your body forwards faster.

You should keep your upper body relaxed when running. Keep your head still but without tension in your neck. Your eye line should be focused gently along the horizon (about 20-30 metres ahead of you). Keep your face and, in particular, your jaw relaxed.

Keep your shoulders relaxed (resist tensing up and pushing them towards your ears) and your upper body lifted nice and tall above the hips, so as not to restrict breathing. Try not to bend forwards from the hips or sink into the hips, as both can cause lower back pain.

Your arms should be held at a 90-degree angle with your hands held in a soft fist with your thumb gently resting on your forefingers. Avoid holding a clenched fist as the tension will spread through the whole upper body. A good way to relax this area is to imagine you are gently holding a thin piece of paper between your thumb and first finger. The movement of your arms should be forwards and backwards with no lateral movement; any side movement will cause a very uneconomical running action.

To prevent injury it is also worth engaging your pelvic floor muscles (this is best described as the muscle group which you use to stop yourself going to the toilet). Gently squeeze these muscles (around 30 per cent effort), as this will help activate your core muscles which will in turn support your back and reduce the risk of injury. Using your pelvic floor muscles is definitely one

to practice in your core and cross-training sessions.

As you can see, the key to correct technique in the upper body is to relax and not carry tension. Many runners, in their determination to go quicker, keep their upper body very stiff, but this tension is energy sapping and unproductive. As with most of your running form, practice makes perfect. So, when you are out training it is worth spending a couple of sessions really focusing on your upper body and maintaining a smooth, easy, relaxed movement.

It is worth noting that many fast runners break technique rules, notably with the upper body. The distinctive running style of marathon runner Paula Radcliffe, whose head bobs about, clearly isn't from the running textbook. Coaches have almost certainly tried to prevent this head movement in the past, but forcing a technique that is supposed to help you run faster can sometimes cause a lot of tension and actually have the opposite effect. The most important thing is to keep relaxed and have a smooth, easy style.

✓ Keep your face relaxed

✗ Do not tense up and hold your jaw in a fixed position

✓ Keep your arms swinging gently forwards and backwards

✗ Don't have any lateral movement

✓ Keep your pelvic floor muscles gently engaged

✗ Do not clench your hands

✓ Keep your body tall over your hips

✗ Do not lean forward

Lower body

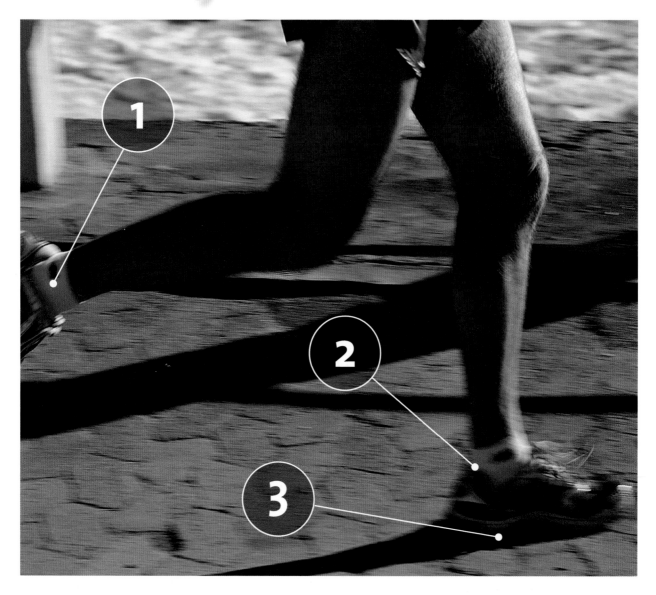

1 Kick your back heel up to your backside.

2 Don't allow your ankle or knee joints to roll too far in or out.

3 Concentrate on having minimal contact time with the surface of the ground.

The work the lower body performs in endurance runs is immense. Therefore, the more economical your action is, the less energy you will expend, and the less chance there is of incurring an injury. Your leg action or running gait can be very hard to change, and you will find that most runners will revert to type. The more you run the more you will naturally find yourself become smoother in your action and covering greater distances with less effort. However, there are some fundamentals which everyone should take notice of.

✓ Kick your heel up towards your backside

✗ Don't have a high knee lift

✓ Wear the correct footwear to avoid injury

✗ Watch out for over-pronating or supinating

✓ Aim for minimal contact time with the ground

✗ Don't place your foot down heavily

✓ Practice your running form in training runs

✗ Don't feel tension in your running form

It's obviously difficult to look at your own running form but it's important you can see your own style because you will immediately be able to pick up some pointers for improvement. The ideal way to do this is to get a friend to film you as you run. If you can't arrange this then you can see your style by running on a treadmill in front of a mirror or alternatively simply go running on a sunny day and look down at the shape and movement of your shadow.

Your back heel should kick up towards your backside. This will maximize the use of your hamstrings and glutes and will also propel your leg forward. Note, this running action is different from that of sprinters who bring their knees up high in front of the body. For most longer distance races the back heel will not need to kick too high, but even a small amount of backlift towards your backside will give you a more efficient running style.

Being light on your feet and minimizing contact time with the surface of the ground is also important. Although when running at a slower pace you will have more contact time, still concentrate on a feeling

of lightness as you cover the ground. Think of gliding across the surface rather than planting each foot down heavily.

You should also be aware of how your feet land on the surface – because as a runner they are going to be doing it lots of times.

Pronation is the inward movement of the foot after it has made contact with the ground. Pronation is a normal part of the running gait and assists in the shock absorption process. Problems can occur when over-pronating (excessive pronation), which can lead to injuries in the knees, ankle joints or even in the back.

The opposite of pronating is supination, which is where the ankle rolls outwards. Again, supination is part of the gait cycle and the shock absorption process, but over-supination can also lead to injury. The easiest correction for both of these problems is to have the correct footwear (see Equipment on pages 20-25).

Foot strike

1 Front-of-foot landing gives a good running form, but it has less shock absorption and will put a large amount of pressure on your calves.

2 Heel strike gives good shock absorption, but is often seen in slower runners and those who over-stride.

3 Mid-foot runners enjoy a good balance of shock absorption and speed.

For most runners the best option with foot strike is to keep your natural style and allow your body to adapt as you run more. However, it is important to know which form you are adopting so you can adapt your stretching sessions accordingly. You will also need to change your foot strike if you are picking up re-occurring injuries.

The heel-coming-down-first style provides the best shock absorption, stretches out the calf muscles and will put less stress on your Achilles tendon. This style is quite body friendly but it is synonymous with slower running, poor backlift and over-striding. You will see a lot of straight-leg runners with a heavy heel strike.

Putting the front of your foot down first can help produce a more economical and faster running style. This is partly because you spend less time with your feet on the floor and it naturally leads to kicking your back heel up towards your backside. This style will also put less stress on your ankles and knees. Runners who use this style tend not to over-stride and place their foot directly under their hips. The main problem with this approach is that the calf muscle is continually contracted and never gets stretched out. This is a major problem if you

are running for four or five hours and will contribute to shin splints, Achilles tendinitis and muscle pulls. Some runners who naturally put the front of their foot down first have also suffered with ITB problems. If you are a front-foot runner and you find it difficult to change then you should incorporate extra stretching sessions, with the main focus on the calf muscles and ITB. Along with regular sports massages, this can help prevent further injuries.

Mid-foot running, as you would expect, gives you some of the advantages

and disadvantages of the other two styles. So, you get a slight calf stretch with not too much pressure on the Achilles tendon and the ITB. However, you do get less absorption than on a heel-strike action. This can cause more problems in the longer races, simply because you are on your feet for longer and are putting more impact on your body for a longer period of time.

✓ Learn which part of the foot you are landing on first

✗ Do not try to change your foot strike overnight

✓ Incorporate the correct stretching for your particular running style

✗ Don't ignore pains – it could lead to further injury

✓ Have a light easy contact with the floor

✗ Avoid a heavy heel strike and straight-legged running

✓ Place your foot directly under your centre of gravity

✗ Do not overstride

Cadence

1 Concentrate on powering off your leg – this is what increases your speed.

2 Place your foot directly under your hips.

3 Concentrate on moving your energy forwards and not up and down.

Some aspects of technique are best left alone. This would be true of your running cadence (amount of strides per minute), but not with where your foot lands.

Your foot should land directly under your hips (your centre of gravity) as this prevents over-striding, which can cause injuries. This problem is normally associated with runners trying to run quicker. If you take longer stride lengths you will find yourself travelling faster. You will also find yourself picking up injuries such as sore knees, pulled glute and hamstring muscles, and the most common injury from regularly over-striding – shin splints.

If you watch most elite athletes the foot lands under the gravity of their body and the amount of strides they take – around 175 to 185 strides per minute (around 90 steps per leg) – is not too dissimilar to many recreational runners. So why are they going faster? The reason is because the power these runners use to push off from their legs is greater, so they will have less contact time with the floor. This means that per stride their body is travelling further, even if the foot landing is in a similar position to a social runner.

You can do an experiment of counting your strides per minute in your warm-up and then when you are running at a faster pace. Most people will find that they are using the same amount of foot strikes. As you progress through your training and you find yourself running faster this leg pace should remain the same. You will feel yourself getting stronger and pushing off your legs harder and thus covering more distance per stride.

Be aware that if you are getting muscle pulls in your glutes or back of your legs then you are probably over-striding so make sure you are not placing the foot in front of your line of gravity. To get extra pace concentrate on pushing off your legs harder, kick your back heel towards your backside and have as little contact time with the ground as possible. You should imagine gliding across the surface and avoid bobbing up and down. You want your energy moving forwards, not up and down.

✓ Place your landing foot under your centre of gravity (your hips)

✗ Do not overstride

✓ Keep your cadence at roughly the same pace

✗ Do not increase the amount of strides in an attempt to go faster

✓ To increase your pace kick your back heel up higher

✗ Do not bob up and down

✓ To increase pace have less contact time with the ground

✗ Do not shuffle your feet

Pacing

1 Don't start too quickly. Be patient and let your early excitement die down.

2 Adjust your pace for the conditions and slow down when running up hills and into headwinds.

3 Aim to run negative splits so you run the first half of the race slightly slower than the second half.

The pacing for a 10 km race and a marathon is surprisingly different, with very different intensity levels from the outset. Pacing is vital to achieve the targets you have set yourself; go off too hard and you will be unable to sustain your target pace but start too slowly and you will never make up the lost time.

10 km

This is probably the longest distance where the pace feels uncomfortable from the start of the run. You will be running at around 90 per cent of your aerobic capacity so make sure you do a full warm-up before the race. Your first kilometre should be slightly slower than the others. As an example, if you are aiming for a 60-minute finish time the first kilometre would be about 20 seconds off pace. You will then need to ease up to slightly faster than your average pace (six minutes per kilometre) to hit your target. Some runners prefer to get straight into their average pace (or even start with a quick kilometre) but for most it is better to ease into the race and make up those few seconds later. The middle part of the race is the toughest because you will be feeling the pace but are still a long way from home. Just be patient and maintain your speed – the kilometres will

pass quickly. As you head towards the finish you need to assess your energy levels. This is the time you need to decide to speed up and really push for a good time or accept you will simply need to fight to sustain your pace. No two races are the same and you need to realize you won't be able to kick for home every time. The benefit of the 10 km race is that you can do quite a few races in a season. Evaluate how you felt and learn from your mistakes.

Half- and full marathons

You need to start these runs slowly. If everyone else is

charging past you at the start then you are going at the correct pace. Don't let this worry you. One of the biggest reasons runners fail to achieve their targets is because they start too fast. Your aim should be to run a negative split (ie the second half of the race should be slightly faster than the first). During the first third of the race you should feel comfortable and for the full marathon it might even feel slow. But once you get into your running stride you can start to hit an even intensity level. You will need to make adjustments for the conditions, so slow down on the uphills, speed up going down, and if it is windy slow down running into it and push on with the tailwind.

✓ Keep your intensity levels even

✗ Do not change intensity levels – it is hard work for your body to keep adjusting effort levels

✓ If it feels everyone is running past you at the start you have got it right

✗ Do not start too quickly

✓ Slow down on the uphills

✗ Do not try to maintain your pace up the hills

✓ You need to get straight into your stride in 10 km races

✗ Do not go out too fast in the half-marathon and marathon

Uphill

1 Pumping your arms on uphills gets the blood flowing and can help to clear lactic acid in your system.

2 Keep an easy relaxed running style and accept you will have to slow down on uphills.

3 Maintain your technique of placing your foot directly under your body and don't over-stride in an effort to get the hill out of the way.

The biggest mistake you can make when running uphill is to tense up. Few people relish hills but they are a part of running. Relax your upper body, don't over-stride, keep your arms moving forwards and backwards and concentrate on keeping your back heel kicking up. If you keep looking forward it will help you avoid tensing up, although some runners prefer to look down at the road so psychologically they can't see the hill ahead. Some runners also take smaller strides and pump their arms a little harder on uphills. This can get the blood flowing and help clear out the lactic acid.

Common errors on uphills are to lean forward and stride out further. This is often done in an attempt to speed up on the hills and get it over and done with. Keep your running form the same easy and relaxed style. The biggest adjustments you should make when running hills is your pacing and mental approach. Are you one of those people who dreads the thought of running up hills? By adjusting your pacing they will feel a lot easier.

The first thing to remember is that your body operates better if you keep it working at an even intensity level. You expend a lot of energy if you keep pushing the intensity up and down. To keep the intensity level you will need to run slower uphill. Your natural instinct will be to push hard to get to the top then ease off the intensity. Although you may be maintaining an even pace your intensity levels (heart-rate levels) are going higher on the uphills. A heart-rate monitor will enable you to check that your heart rate stays within five beats per minute of its level when you are running on the flat (although this does depend on the gradient and length of the hill).

Bear in mind an even approach is right for race day but not always for training, where you can push yourself up the hills. Working the hills hard will improve lactic thresholds, strength in your legs and your mental strength. You should also make certain that you run completely over the top of the hill and keep working yourself for another 50 metres.

A common error in hill training is to get to the peak exhausted and slow down. By keeping your pace even for that extra distance you will be giving yourself a more gradual lowering in intensity (which can prevent you feeling light headed). It will also give you extra mental strength so when it comes to race day you won't just ease off when you get to the top of a hard hill. This is the time you want to push a little harder in the race.

So the key to your hills is to keep your form even, keep your intensity levels even and learn to embrace the challenge. Hill running is excellent for increasing strength in your legs and mind and this will ultimately help you become a better runner on the flat as well.

✓ Keep your body relaxed

✗ Don't over-stride

✓ Keep looking forward into the distance

✗ Don't push too hard to get up the hill quicker

✓ Embrace the challenge of taking on the hills

✗ Don't fear hills – they are a part of running

✓ Maintain your technique when running uphill

✗ Don't lean forward into the hill

Downhill

1 Try to increase your leg speed when running downhill.

2 Keep your body perpendicular to the hill.

3 Place your landing foot slightly behind the hip line.

When you are running downhill simply try to think of falling gracefully. Don't force it but instead allow your body to use the gravity to pick up pace as you head for the bottom of the hill and revel in the fact that you are conserving energy by using natural forces.

Running downhill can be very hard on your body, especially your back and knees, which can take a pounding. However, if you keep on fine-tuning your technique you will gain the confidence to really go for it. Then, gradually, you will find yourself running faster downhill, using less effort and not waking up in the morning with aching joints.

When running downhill concentrate on keeping your body perpendicular to the hill and avoid your natural inclination to lean backwards. Leaning back will cause more pressure on your lower back and you will consume more energy.

Keep your body propelling forward and ensure that you keep your posture tall and avoid shuffling your feet. The main difference between running downhill and on the flat is that you should place your foot slightly behind your hips. Instead of the normal technique of placing your foot directly under your hips it should land slightly behind your hip line to reduce some of the impact, allowing you to fully utilize the momentum of the hill.

Many runners also increase their cadence (leg speed) on the downhill as this can lessen the impact on joints and increase pace at the same time. This is a technique to practise, as you may feel out of control on the descent when you first do this. At first you may feel like an elephant tumbling down the hill but over time you will feel as if you are skipping across the surface and benefiting from the momentum of the slope.

A lot of these techniques require a bit of faith and confidence in your ability. It is natural to put the brakes on when running downhill. Practice each technique a little at a time and you will slowly find yourself making up great time during the race overall.

When running downhill always be aware of the terrain you are running on. As you are running quite fast and pushing it hard so that you are almost out of control it will be hard to make sudden stops. Be aware of what is out in front of you, such as potholes, roads bisecting your route or any other obstacles which you may need to avoid.

If you have got your pacing up the hill correct then you will have some energy to really work a little harder when running downhill. Most runners, when they are starting out, will push too hard up the hills, then not work hard enough downhill.

✓ Think of falling gracefully when running downhill

✗ Don't shuffle your feet

✓ Increase your cadence

✗ Don't slow down

✓ Place your landing foot slightly behind the hip line

✗ Be careful not to over-stride

✓ Keep the body perpendicular to the hill

✗ Don't lean backwards

The dark

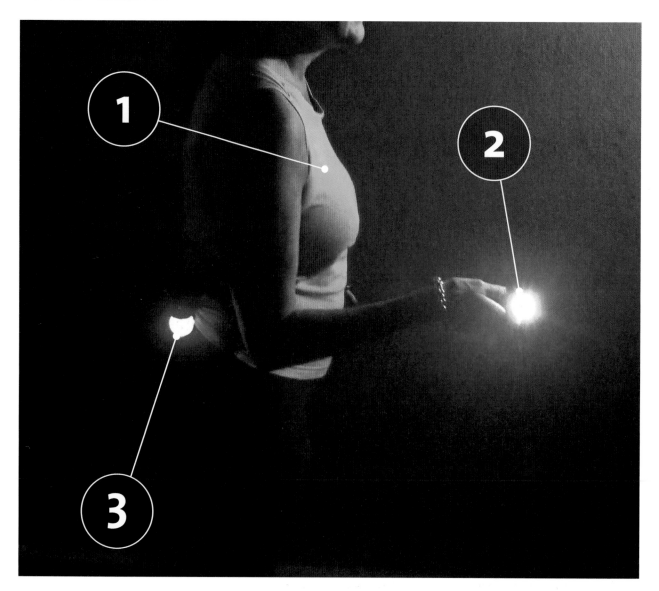

1 Wear a bright top so you can be seen (when the car headlights shine on you!).

2 A small hand torch can help you see where you are going, as well as showing other road users you are there.

3 Wear a red flashing light on your back so traffic can see you easily.

When running in the dark the main consideration is safety. The most important thing is what you are wearing. You need to be seen, so a high-visibility running top or jacket is a must. If you are running in a well-lit area with pavements then a bright jacket should be enough. However, dark comes down quicker than you might expect so think ahead. Avoid wearing black if you think your run might head into the dark part of the day, especially if you know it's an area with no street lamps or pavements, which can be made worse by a poor road surface that you

won't be able to see. The headlights of the cars are especially dangerous because you can be blinded by the beams. If you find yourself in a difficult situation as the day turns to night simply slow down and keep safe; you can always run tomorrow.

But if you plan ahead there is no reason why you can't hit the road at night and still have a good run. As well as a bright jacket, options are a hand torch and a back light on your jacket or attached to a bag if carrying one (you can use a flashing red cycle light). You should also make your moving parts visible: reflector wrist or ankle bands will help car drivers to establish that you are a runner. You may feel like you are lit up like a Christmas tree, but it is more important to be safe.

To help you see where you are going you will need a hand torch. You can get very light, small but powerful torches (about the size of two small batteries), which if directed diagonally downwards will help you to see any potholes or other potential dangers.

If you are running in the dark on the road then run on the side of the road facing the oncoming traffic. Remember

to keep the beam of your hand torch pointing down but bear in mind that the drivers of the cars heading towards you may not give you the same courtesy when it comes to dipping their lights.

✓ Wear a brightly coloured jacket whenever running at night

✗ Do not go out for your run dressed in all black

✓ In dark lanes you will need a hand torch to help you monitor the way ahead

✗ Be careful not to shine a bright torch at the windscreen of oncoming traffic

✓ Have a flashing red light attached to your clothing or bag on your back

✗ Do not keep running if the traffic is dangerous; step aside and let it pass

Wet and other weather conditions

1 A lightweight jacket will keep you warm and dry before the race starts. A bin liner also does the trick and can be thrown away.

2 Wear light clothing when it's raining as you will get wet anyway and heavy clothes will just hold the water and weigh you down.

3 Shorten your strides in particularly wet areas of the course as this will reduce your chance of slipping.

Wet

Don't worry about getting wet because your skin is waterproof. If it is raining heavily then whatever you wear is eventually going to get wet so you might as well wear light clothing to start with. If you wear material that holds water you are not only going to get wet but it will also get heavier throughout the run. To keep dry and warm before the start you can wear a lightweight jacket (which you will need to carry through the race) or a bin liner which you can throw away.

Cold

There is some great running kit on the market that will keep you warm while drawing the moisture away from your body. When going out for a training run in the cold wrap up quite warm. If you wear gloves and a hat (preferably bright in colour), you can often still run in a light long sleeve top and shorts for runs of up to 90 minutes. However for those long three to four hour slow runs, you might want to add running tights and a light running jacket because your intensity level will be a lot lower.

When running a race you will be working harder so you should keep warm from the run itself – gloves, a light long sleeve top and shorts should be enough. If you are unsure then it is a good idea to wear some warm clothes that you don't mind throwing away if you find yourself getting too hot. This is more of a consideration for the bigger events, as you will have to line-up earlier and will be standing around in cold weather for a long time. Remember that if you are a slower runner then you will be out on the road for longer so you may need a bit more clothing to see you through.

Snow and ice

You will need to be very careful on your foot placement if running on ice. Ideally it's best to not even run as the lack of grip makes it impossible to push off properly and the chances of falling are high. On very snowy days you can stick to the fields and as long as the snow is not too deep you will find that the softer surface of the fields means it should not be too slippery. You will find that you will be running a lot slower but you will also be surprised at what a great workout you will get, as your body, especially your legs, will have to work much harder.

Sun

The main thing when running in the sun is to use sun block. Use a high factor as you will not be able to reapply and will be sweating a lot of it off your body during the race. It is best to put the sun block on one hour before you set off so it can soak into the skin (read the manufactures guidelines as each will vary). Sunglasses are a big benefit, especially as you get tired during the long races and a hat will keep the sun off your head and face if it has a peak.

✔ Do wear sun block on sunny days

✗ Don't wear heavy clothing when it's raining

✔ Keep yourself dry and warm before the start with a bin liner or lightweight jacket

✗ Don't wear a heavy jacket you are going to have to carry for the rest of the event

✔ Do wrap up a bit more on cold days for the long slow runs

✗ Don't worry too much about the rain; your skin is waterproof

Big events

1 Big events can have a lot of congestion, making it hard to achieve time targets.

2 Pick and choose carefully when to overtake as you do not want to run further than necessary.

3 If you want to slow down or stop then get yourself to the edge of the course so you do not cause a collision.

When choosing your target time you need to be realistic as to what is achievable for that particular course. If you are looking to run a personal best then choosing a very congested race is not advisable. For example, in the UK, the Great North Run is a fantastic half-marathon event, full of vibrancy and colour but it is so congested that many runners fall below their expectations when it comes to their finish time.

It doesn't mean you shouldn't enter these big events because they are a lot of fun and a great experience, but unless you are an elite runner or a celebrity, with a clear route, you must accept that you will be slowed down by periods of congestion. There are many smaller marathons throughout the world without this problem. These events, though, tend not to have the same water and sports drinks provided, so be careful to check what they provide on the course.

Most 10 km runs don't have too much congestion once you get past the start line. This is probably because you have a greater range of speeds among runners from the very outset. The main problems arise in the half- and full marathons, especially if you are trying to complete a common time target (eg 4 hours) where you will find

yourself running with a large group of runners who are all attempting the same time.

If you find yourself in a lot of congestion you need to make a choice. Is the congestion slowing you up so much that you will never make up the time? By weaving in and out of runners are you going to get a clear run, or just find yourself at the same pace five metres further up the field? When you overtake other runners you might be running a lot further than necessary and in the marathon in particular you

✓ Do choose a smaller race if you are going for a PB

✗ Do not aim for a PB in the big events as there will be too much congestion

✓ Be patient in the big events and enjoy the occasion

✗ Do not use up valuable energy weaving in and out of the crowds; carefully choose when to overtake

✓ Be aware of running too close behind other runners, especially towards the end of a marathon when people tend to stop and walk

✗ Do not just stop in the centre of the running lanes

really need to conserve energy for the task at hand. Generally you are better staying in the group and waiting for the congestion to clear as it usually does. It is also worth noting that if you do need to stop or slow down then make sure no one is running at pace behind you and try to get to the edges of the course so you don't have anyone running into the back of you.

It can be difficult to get an entry place in many of the big events (the London Marathon ballot gives you a one-in-five chance of entry for instance). The other option is to gain a place through a charity. Many big events do a wonderful job in rasing money for charity so check the organiser's website for any charities looking for entrants, as in general they will guarantee you a place in return for you raising a certain amount of money for their charity. Another option is to gain a place through the 'good for age' route. Most big races will have set times per age group and if you can prove you have achieved that time within a certain time frame you may be able to gain entry through that route.

fitness & training

// FASTER // FITTER // MORE MOTIVATED

Training zones

Training zones allow you to work at the correct intensity. When starting a training session it is important to know the reason you are training. What is your goal for this session and what do you want your mind and body to achieve? It is unrealistic to think that you can push your body 100 per cent every time you hit the road. This is why training programmes start with a light workload and then have gradual increases. Even as the workload increases there will still be some lighter weeks that allow your body to recover.

A lot of your planning will depend on your training history. If you have prepared for an event before you will be more aware of what your body can sustain without suffering adverse affects. If this is the first time you are undertaking a more structured training programme, or if you are training for a new event, you should try to follow the training programme you set out and take care not to get carried away (See Over-training and over-reaching on page 56).

There are also many positive aspects for working at the correct intensities. Improving different areas of training zones will enable you to get faster and stronger for longer periods, both mentally and

physically. Working in the correct training zones allows you, even if you are training by yourself with little or no support, to prepare as the professionals do.

A lot of what we set out in this section is based around heart-rate monitors. If you are training without a heart-rate monitor, then you will need to use what we call Rate of Perceived Exertion (RPE). Imagine a scale of one to 10. One is little or no effort, while 10 would be your maximum effort. Where a heart-rate percentage is displayed, simply divide the figure by 10 to get the correct figure for yourself (eg 70-80 per cent of maximum heart rate would equate to 7-8 RPE).

Your heart-rate monitor will normally work out correct training intensities automatically for you. The equation below is included for those monitors that don't and also so you have some background information as to what the monitors are doing.

220 - your age - your resting heart rate. Intensity per cent + resting heart rate = target training zone

For example: an athlete who is aged 30 and has a resting heart rate of 70 beats per minute (bpm) training at 60 per cent

of maximum heart rate will be calculated as follows:

220 - 30 - 70 = 120
70 per cent of 120 = 84 + 70 = 154 bpm

It is important to remember that you know your body better than your heart-rate monitor so if you are feeling very ill or dizzy and your heart rate is still low you may need to listen to your body, take down the intensity or even stop. You should also be aware that before aiming for your target training zones you should you be fully warmed up and allow time for your heart rate to climb to the training levels.

Endurance work
60-75 per cent of maximum heart rate

This intensity will normally make up the bulk of your work. You may also hear this referred to as the fat-burning zone, base training or train don't strain. With good technique and an injury-free body you should be able to sustain long periods of time in this training zone.

At this lower intensity level your body can cope with large volumes of time training. Your body should not be put under too much strain, allowing you to concentrate on perfecting technique. It is in this

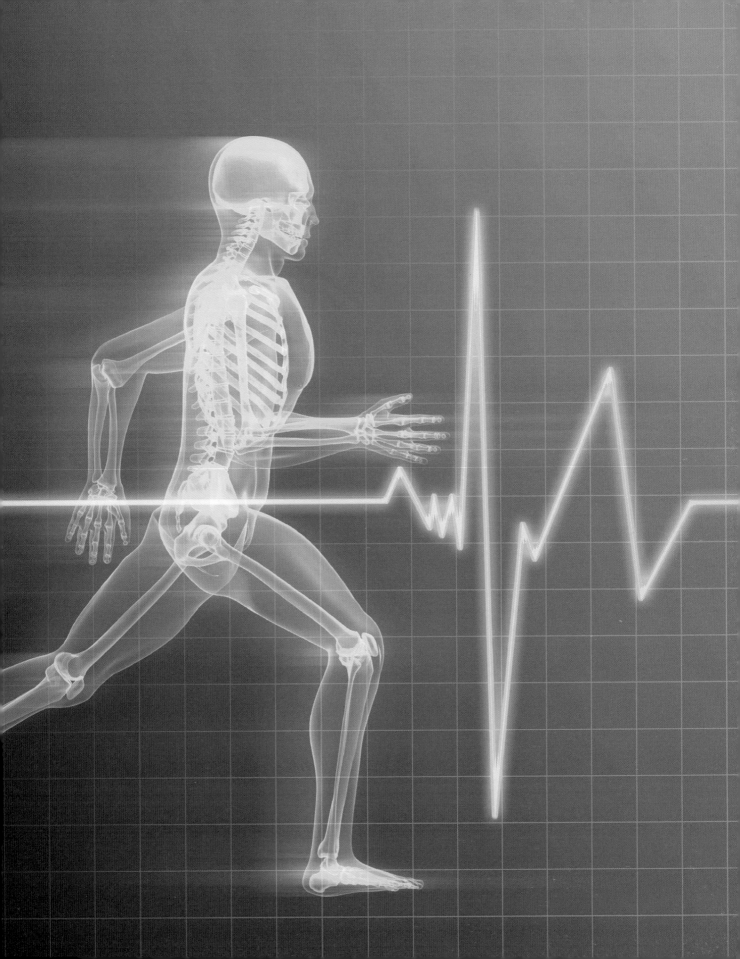

zone that you will be putting in the long hours on the road and this creates a really good base for your training as well as your body. Physically your body benefits from a stronger heart, the increased ability to take oxygen on-board and using this oxygen more efficiently to help the body perform better. By constantly repeating the correct running action your muscles will soon remember what to do and in times of fatigue this can really help to sustain good technique, which will maximize speed and efficiency.

It is also in this training zone that your body will burn high levels of fat. By working at the lower intensity levels the main source of energy your body uses will be fat. Because you can sustain this lower level for longer periods of time and your main fuel is body fat, this equates to a lot of body-fat burning.

This is good news for most people and it can be very rewarding to see your body-fat percentage lower, as well as making you a better performer. After a sustained period of training sessions you will also notice that you can run further while keeping your heart rate in the same training zone. For some people this happens remarkably fast and it can be really motivating to see the rewards so quickly.

Anaerobic/lactate thresholds
80-90 per cent of maximum heart rate

The above percentages really are just a guideline. The only way to truly establish your exact lactate thresholds is to be tested in a lab. Obviously many of us do not have this option as it can be expensive and requires taking blood.

Your next best option is to do a time trial of your own. Set a distance that is challenging to complete over a 30-minute period and then take your average heart rate over this period. If you feel halfway through the run that you cannot continue due to muscle fatigue, or your muscles are 'burning', stop and see what your heart rate is as this can be a good indicator as to your lactate threshold.

What's happening and why does it matter? Without becoming too complicated, when training at these levels of intensity, the main source of energy used is glycogen (which is stored in the muscles). A by-product of this is the release of lactate acid. Once this lactate acid accumulates to a certain level your performance will become greatly reduced. So by training at the correct levels it is possible to increase your thresholds and your body can then deal with

the release of the lactate acid more efficiently.

This type of training can greatly enhance your performance. Although it will be less in volume to the endurance work, training around these thresholds can give you the ability to cover longer distances at a faster pace with a lower heart rate. This lower heart rate means that you will produce less lactate acid and can continue with less muscle fatigue. You will be greatly surprised at the gains your body can make in these training levels.

Red-line zone
90-100 per cent of maximum heart rate

This zone is rarely used for endurance athletes. It is mainly used for speed and interval training and can only be sustained for short periods, even if you are very fit. Points to note are that the heart rate can be increased by other factors and may cause you to adjust your training zones accordingly. Dehydration, heat and altitude can all cause the heart rate to increase anywhere between seven to 10 per cent.

Over-training and over-reaching

The sensation of fatigue is necessary because it lets you know you are pushing your physical limits. You train to improve your performance and your body generally reacts positively to being 'pushed'. However, in certain circumstances, if your body is over-stimulated or stimulated incorrectly, you will suffer adverse effects.

Levels of fatigue

1. The first level of fatigue is hypoglycaemia – the term for abnormally low levels of blood glucose. You reach this when you have exhausted your glycogen stores, haven't ingested enough carbohydrates to produce more blood glucose and are still running.
2. Post-training fatigue is the natural response to several hours of intense exercise, which tells you that you are pushing your normal training limits.
3. Over-reaching is the next step up and is when short-term performance drops and develops as a result of an intense training session. Symptoms are those of normal fatigue. The right amount of recovery will allow you to become faster and stronger. It is, however, a warning.
4. Over-training is the debilitating and long-term (often lasting weeks and sometimes months)

fatigue, which degrades rather than stimulates performance.

Over-training in volume and/or intensity can lead to some inevitable outcomes. Firstly, if you train too hard or over-train, your immune system will be very low, leaving you susceptible to illness. A cold can set you back a long way in your preparation. You would be amazed at what lengths top endurance athletes go to avoid illness.

The other potential problem you face is injury. Over-use of your muscles in the gym or on the road, where you are repeating the same action over and over again, can lead to those all too familiar injury problems for runners, around the shins and the knees.

Burnout is another key issue to consider. If you keep pushing your body as hard as you can in every session for as long as you can, you will eventually find yourself not wanting to train. Having a different target for each session will help you stay mentally prepared for each run.

How to prevent over-training

The most frequent causes of over-training are: excessive increase in training loads, insufficient recovery periods, poor diet (insufficient quantity of carbohydrates or other

nutritional elements), travel factors and a lack of variety in your training.

So how do you prevent over-training? You need a balance between training and recovery both at long term (mesocycle) and short term (microcycle). This means that after a few weeks of heavy training, the intensity should be reduced for a period of time (usually a week) and the number of rest days should be increased. The purpose of this recovery week is to allow your body complete regeneration.

Most training programmes include one or two rest days per week as well as a day or two of easy running, allowing you to recover. Unvaried training programmes without alternating periods of high and low volume/intensity also severely increase the risk of over-training. The key is planning your own personal training programme to occasionally over-reach but not over-train. Your challenge is finding your own individual boundary.

Mental strength

It is said success in sport is determined 90 per cent by fitness and skill (physiology, biomechanics, etc) and 10 per cent by mental strength. This 10 per cent is significant and can play a massive part in helping you to improve performance and extract more enjoyment from sport. It is an area that until quite recently was largely ignored by the sporting community but these days it is widely recognized as a key tool in every sportsperson's kit bag.

Developing your mental strength will help improve motivation and confidence, both during training (oh, those cold winter mornings!) and on race day. It will also help you perform better under pressure, including keeping any emotional distractions in check. You should ignore this part of your training programme at your peril; you could significantly compromise all your hard training if you haven't prepared mentally for an event.

Why only train your body when your mind needs training, too?

So how can 'mental strength' be measured? Obviously, this is difficult to do, and is quite subjective, but it is possible by answering a few key questions to work out your mental strength rating. Among these are (measure on a scale of one to five):

Mark one to five in the boxes below

☐ What is my current level of self-confidence?

☐ How much mental preparation do I commit to prior to an event?

☐ Do I always learn something, new or old, from my hard training sessions or races?

☐ Do I continually stretch targets for myself, both in training and racing?

☐ How good do I consider my levels of concentration to be, both during training and racing?

☐ How relaxed am I before an event?

☐ Do I forgive myself when things don't go quite according to plan?

☐ How well do I control negative thoughts?

☐ Do I feel I get the most enjoyment out of training and racing?

☐ How much do I enjoy the competitive element of racing?

Note any question where you recorded a score of three or less; these are the areas that perhaps need a little attention in terms of improving mental fitness. Most of these areas are covered later, with suggestions on how improvements could be made.

It is an undisputed fact that the workings of the mind and the body are linked – how you feel undoubtedly affects performance. Keeping the mind in tune with the body maximizes the possibility that improved performances can be achieved, and maintaining a positive mental attitude will soon bring results.

So how can we mentally prepare for training and racing? Much has been written about goal setting in sports and there is a very good reason for that: it works! The process of goal setting is designed to help increase confidence and motivation, which in turn will help improve performance. Most people are excellent at setting goals; sadly less of us are as good at achieving them. You have only got to look at New Year resolutions for that. So, why is this? Part of the reason is that many people have no focus to their goals but tend to choose things they feel they ought to do, rather than the things they want to do, or the things that motivate them. Also, they tend not to have any structure to their goals, which leads to a lack of focus and

direction, and eventually they can peter out.

Many runners will be aware of the SMART approach to goal setting. SMART stands for Specific, Measureable, Achievable, Relevant and Time bound. This structure has been used for many years as a way of ensuring individual's goals are fit for purpose. However, this can be expanded into SCCAMP, which is as follows:

- **Specific.** It is important that goals are specific and clearly understood. Any ambiguity could lead to a loss in focus.
- **Controllable.** Goals should be something within your control; anything which has strong external dependencies could lead to failure.
- **Challenging.** There seems little point in setting goals that can already be achieved. Stretching your targets are the requirement.
- **Achievable.** Again, there is little point in having a target that is always likely to be out of reach, such as running a marathon in under an hour. Unachievable goals are likely to demotivate.
- **Measureable.** If a goal is not measureable how will you know you have achieved it?
- **Personal.** The more meaning the goal has, the more you will be

driven to achieve it (eg proving detractors wrong!). *"I was told when I was 18 that I was too small to be a good 800 m runner. I rather enjoyed proving them wrong there."* Seb (now Lord) Coe.

When developing goals, it is important to consider the type of goals that are likely to satisfy your overall objective of improving performance, namely outcome goals and performance goals. An example of an outcome goal could be "I want to finish in the top 50 of the next 10 km race I enter." Unfortunately you probably have no control over such a conclusion, as this could influenced by a whole host of external factors, and failing to achieve such a goal could lead to you becoming demotivated. It is better to set performance goals, where you do have control over the outcome, such as: "I want to be relaxed throughout, to keep focused, and to complete the race strongly."

It is essential you write these goals down and refer to them regularly. This will help provide a consistent link between what you are doing physically and what your ultimate aims are mentally. In addition, setting goals will set your subconscious to attract things that will support the goal.

The specificity of your goals can further be defined by the horizon you are choosing for your goals. A good tip is to maintain a multi-horizon set of objectives. For instance, choose two or three at 30 days ahead, a similar number at six months and perhaps a third set for 12 months. As each horizon approaches the detail for each goal becomes increasingly specific and a constant strategy for improvement is executed. Apply this across both training programmes and races.

Two of the most important areas of mental fitness are motivation (being motivated, maintaining it, regaining it) and confidence, which is defined as 'a feeling of self-assurance arising from one's appreciation of one's own abilities or qualities'. These two areas contribute more to mental fitness than any other and it is by paying particular attention to these areas that significant performance improvements can be achieved.

But what is motivation? It is defined as 'a drive to fulfil a need'. Motivation drives us to do things; it is important because it energises and directs our behaviour. Motivation is actually a personality trait and there are two main types – motive to avoid failure (in other words avoid tasks which could be measured as failure by others) and a motive to achieve success. An example of motivation in a sporting context would be a penalty shoot-out in football. Some players are motivated to achieve the success of scoring a penalty, others are motivated by the fact they really don't want to miss (fail).

Of course, there comes a time when everyone's motivation starts to wane a little and it is important to recognize that this is likely to happen to you, particularly during long training sessions between competitive races. So what can you do? Try a few of these ideas:

• Keep an eye on your sleep levels. Increasing the amount of sleep can improve performance and assist recovery. Physical training takes its toll on body and mind and both need to properly recover
• Cross training helps relieve boredom and burnout. Rest days and light training days also help maintain a healthy mental state
• Listening to music relaxes and empowers. Or perhaps try watching sport recordings for inspiration and technique
• Consider meditation which will certainly help focus and concentration
• Revisit your purpose. If you ask "Why?" enough you will be able to return to your inner values.

Maintaining a positive mental attitude also helps to maintain healthy motivation levels, particularly during a tough training session or race. Thoughts in your head will influence you, so it is surely better to keep more positive thoughts in the head than negative ones? The conscious mind has difficulty processing negation. If I ask you not to think of the colour blue, you have to think of the colour blue to process the information.

The use of imagery techniques will help maintain a positive approach, particularly for a race event. Try the following:

• Imagine yourself at an event, just before the start, feeling relaxed and positive and confident.
• Use all your senses to obtain a full all-round 'image' of the day. Imagery is sometimes referred to as 'visualization', but this infers the use of a single sense so I prefer the term imagery, which allows the use of all the senses. 'See' the other competitors lining up, 'hear' the hubbub of the watching crowd, 'feel' the breeze on your face and so on.
• Imagine yourself starting the race, running strongly and confidently, passing other runners, feeling happy and in control as the race progresses.

• If you are aware of any steep hills on the course, imagine yourself pushing up these, enjoying the burn as you move smoothly along. This is quite important. The conscious mind can sometimes blur an imagined event with a real event, so if you have already 'run' up the steep hill, you know what to expect because you have experienced it already, at least in your mind. This is called a 'future memory'.
• Now, imagine the final stretch, running strongly and confidently up to the finish line, in an excellent time. Give yourself another 'future memory' of someone handing you a well-deserved cold drink (or whatever your usual 'reward' is) at the end of the race!
• Try and run through this imagery a few times before the race. In this way you can be quite prepared for the race itself.
• Some people include minor problems in the imagery race so as to prepare themselves for all eventualities. Perhaps a change in the weather, or a dog on the course, or whatever. This way they will have already 'experienced' the event, and can prepare themselves accordingly.

It is also a good idea to keep a record of your training, using

a diary, focusing on those sessions that you feel most excited about. An easier than expected session, a training PB, a time when you felt really focused and in the zone. Referring to these regularly, particularly just before you go to sleep when your mind is most susceptible to suggestion, will instil a sense of positivity and will also help you to maintain high levels of motivation.

So, we arrive at race day. What kind of things can we exploit to ensure we maximize all that hard physical training and that we really enjoy ourselves on the day? Here are a few ideas for you to try:

- Have a last look at your diary, remind yourself of the excellent training sessions or races you've enjoyed, get yourself feeling relaxed, confident and positive.
- Replay the imagery of the race in your mind again, 'remember' how excellent your run is going to be.
- Don't try to 'eat the elephant', particularly for longer races. By this, I mean break the race up into manageable chunks, and focus on each chunk as you approach it. For example, in a 10 km race focus only on the first 2 km, keep the pace steady, with relaxed breathing, and so on. Then focus on the next 2 km, keep focused on pace and the strategy you

planned before the race. Then the next 2 km, and so on. This can be a powerful tool.
- Use triggers to maintain focus. As we are aware, it is easy to lose concentration during a race, so choose a couple of key words or phrases such as "Push on" or perhaps "Stay relaxed/strong/controlled", and when you repeat them in the race itself they can help trigger the necessary focus.
- If you approach a steep hill, try looking down straight to the ground. By doing this, any gradient is removed from sight (and therefore mind) and covering the ground will look the same as running on the flat so running becomes easier. Of course, you should be sure that no obstacles are coming up and that you have a clear run. Safety should be your priority here.
- Don't beat yourself up about things that don't go to plan. Recognize this has happened, plan to learn from it and move on. Certainly don't let the negativity fester. Remove it and return to a positive mind-set. It is vital to focus on what you can control during a race. If you concern yourself too much with the things that are outside of your influence you will be wasting unnecessary energy and potentially lose focus on the things you can influence.

After the race it is always a good idea to conduct a 'three and three review'. Focus on three things that went well and three that didn't go as planned. In this way, you can remain positive, and take strength from the things that were successful, while not allowing yourself to become complacent but at the same time give yourself something to learn from.

So, after you have spent a little time developing your mental fitness, return to the questionnaire at the beginning and work out your score again. You should see definite improvements in a number of areas, which means you are developing an edge to your running skills that your fellow competitors may lack!

Common running injuries

There are, of course, many different injuries but many can occur because of the repeated nature of your training. You can reduce the risks by following the advice in this book: only gradually increase the time you spend running, stretch after every run and ensure your body is conditioned in the early stages of training by following the strength and cross-training programmes. You should, of course, seek specialist medical advice with all injuries.

Runners' knee

The most common runners' knee injury is felt as pain on the lateral part of the knee. This happens when the iliotibial band (ITB) – thick fibres band running down the side of the leg inserting just below the knee – become tight due to instability around the hip area when running. This tight band then rubs on the outside of the knee causing inflammation. To prevent this make sure you do the ITB stretch (see page 74) after each run and use the exercises to strengthen your glutes (see pages 85, 90, 91, 94, 108). If your glutes are strong and active your pelvis will remain stable when running and prevent the rubbing that causes the inflammation. Short-term treatment and relief is often performed by a physio massaging the band and you can also massage the muscle out using a foam roller.

Plantar fasciitis

The plantar fascia is a connective tissue going from the heel bone to the toes. It is often felt as pain under the foot and in the early stages is felt first thing in the morning as it tightens overnight. It is usually caused by allowing the calf muscles to become tight or wearing the wrong footwear when running so you are over-pronating. To prevent this make sure you regularly stretch your calf muscles, especially after training and see a specialist to assess your footwear and running gait. To treat it you need to rest until the pain has subsided, use an ice or cold compression to reduce inflammation and stretch the plantar fascia.

Achilles tendonitis

The Achilles tendon connects the calf muscles to the heel bone and can provide a lot of the power when you push off the foot when running. An acute (occurring over a period of a few days) case can be felt as pain at the back of the ankle with onset taking a few days, and it is common to feel the pain when you start exercising. Chronic (takes longer for the pain to set in) tendonitis can take months to take hold and you will feel the pain continuing throughout exercise. A chronic case can be particularly painful when walking up and down stairs. This injury is often caused by runners increasing

their running times, distances or hills suddenly. Other causes are weak or tight calf muscles, over-pronation and less recovery time. To prevent the injury only gradually increase the amount of running you do, make sure you have the correct footwear, and keep calf muscles strong and flexible. To treat the injury you need rest and cold compression.

Shin splints

Although many runners complain of shin splints when they first start running they are normally feeling pain at the lower front part of the leg, which can be an adaptation to the running programme. True shin splints are found on the front inside on the shin bone and have a number of causes, such as front foot running (see page 34), heavy landings, incorrect footwear and downhill running (see page 42). Symptoms are pain on the inside of the shin bone, lumps and bumps along the bone in this area, with the pain subsiding when exercising but returning stronger the next day. To treat shin splints, rest with your feet up and put a bag of frozen peas on the area (these are excellent as they mould themselves around the leg). If the injury persists a physio may provide shock absorbers for your shoes or a calf and shin support. Applying heat before training is sometimes recommended.

Stretches

Stretching plays a crucial role in injury prevention and enhancing overall athletic performance and yet it is often overlooked and neglected by many athletes as the 'soft' part of the training programme. Stretching is every bit as important as pushing a big, heavy weight or putting in those extra high-intensity kilometres in your training. Don't miss your stretching regime just to get in a few more minutes hard training. It's the wrong move.

By training regularly you will be shortening certain muscles. To ensure you maintain an equal muscular balance throughout your body it is imperative you do not skip the stretches that help to keep these muscles in shape. Although it is important to stretch before a session to prepare for what is to follow, it is also vital to stretch afterwards as well.

This can be hard to do after a tough session or race but generally athletes should spend a lot longer stretching after a heavy training session than before it. In general, it is best to do your stretching at the end of a workout, stretching out the muscles you have just worked for a minimum of one minute each. This will help prevent the shortening of muscles and muscular imbalances in your body, which can cause pain,

injury and may also stop you from training or competing.

So, for example, if you have performed a set of squats you will need to stretch your quads, hamstrings, glutes, calves and lower back. This is just basic maintenance stretching. When you start to clock up more kilometres in training it is advisable to use your rest days to take deeper and longer stretches. Many people neglect this area of their training. A day off is a day off a lot of us think. But get into the habit of giving those muscles you have worked so hard during the week, a really good stretch. You can also do your maintenance stretches on your rest breaks when training.

For the deeper stretches, which really improve your flexibility and balance, it's advisable to find a suitable yoga or stretch class. Stretching really can make a difference between achieving your goals and failing to get to the start line. Take it seriously and do not think it's just something you need to get out of the way before the serious work: this is part of the serious work.

Consider also that before a training session or important race your stress levels can rise, so before stretching you should consider

paying attention to what most of us take for granted: breathing. Slowly take a couple of long breaths in and out through your nose. Or take one big, deep breath from your stomach. In sport, especially at the highest level, small details can make a significant difference. That's why even a tiny relief from your stress might result in finding just that energy you need even if it's just for a few seconds to help keep you focused and relaxed.

Over the next few pages you will see details of some key stretches. You can use these before and after training/racing but do not neglect to do these stretches on your day off. Also, while these are key stretches for many of the muscles you will use, do not rely on these entirely. Remember to stretch out as many muscles as possible to keep muscular balance.

Stretches – glutes

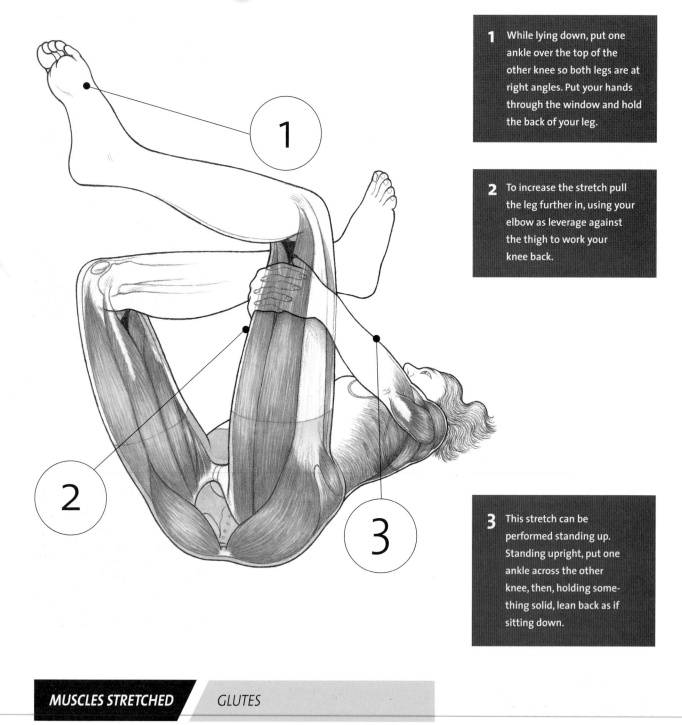

1 While lying down, put one ankle over the top of the other knee so both legs are at right angles. Put your hands through the window and hold the back of your leg.

2 To increase the stretch pull the leg further in, using your elbow as leverage against the thigh to work your knee back.

3 This stretch can be performed standing up. Standing upright, put one ankle across the other knee, then, holding something solid, lean back as if sitting down.

MUSCLES STRETCHED   *GLUTES*

Stretches – seated back twist

1 While sitting down, bend the right leg in front, step the left leg over the top with the knee pointing up to the ceiling and gently twist towards the left. Hold and repeat on the other side.

2 It is very important to keep the lower back straight and your chest expanded. You can hook your elbow over your top knee to increase the stretch.

3 Some people find this stretch awkward. What you can do is straighten the front leg and place the other foot inside the knee, not over the top, as you will find this a little easier.

MUSCLES STRETCHED   *SHOULDERS AND BACK*

Stretches – lower back

1 While lying down bring one knee into your chest with the other leg pointing straight out. Gently pull your knee across your body with the opposite arm and out to the side.

1

2

3

2 Really relax into the stretch, keeping your shoulders on the floor and allowing your abs to soften. Keep your knee high up to your chest.

3 Remember to stretch both sides. You will feel a lot of the tension created from the tough runs ease out of your lower back and glutes.

MUSCLES STRETCHED *LOWER BACK AND GLUTES*

Stretches – hamstring

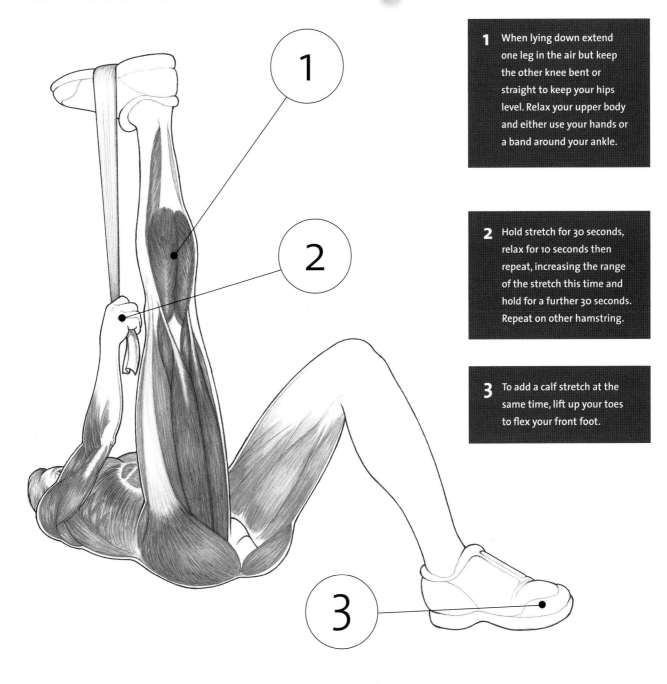

1 When lying down extend one leg in the air but keep the other knee bent or straight to keep your hips level. Relax your upper body and either use your hands or a band around your ankle.

2 Hold stretch for 30 seconds, relax for 10 seconds then repeat, increasing the range of the stretch this time and hold for a further 30 seconds. Repeat on other hamstring.

3 To add a calf stretch at the same time, lift up your toes to flex your front foot.

MUSCLES STRETCHED   *HAMSTRINGS AND CALVES*

Stretches – hip flexor

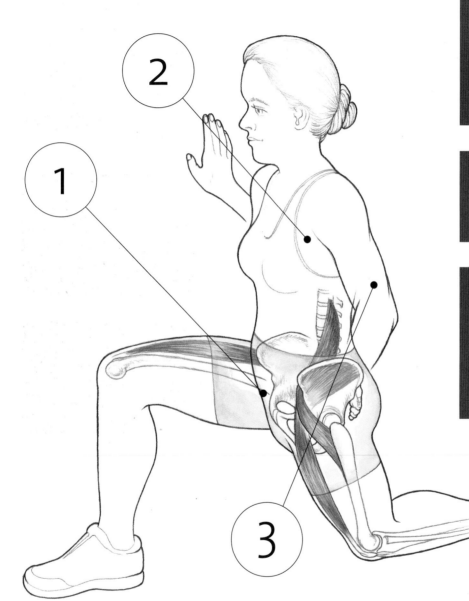

1 While kneeling on one leg ensure both legs are at a right angles. Tuck your pelvis under your leading leg and you will feel a stretch at the top of the thigh.

2 Remember to keep your body lifted to get the most out of the stretch. A common error is to lean forward.

3 Hold this position briefly, then reach up to the ceiling with your arm that is on the side of your back leg and twist away from this arm so you are looking towards your back foot.

MUSCLES STRETCHED   *HIP FLEXORS AND ITB*

Stretches – quads

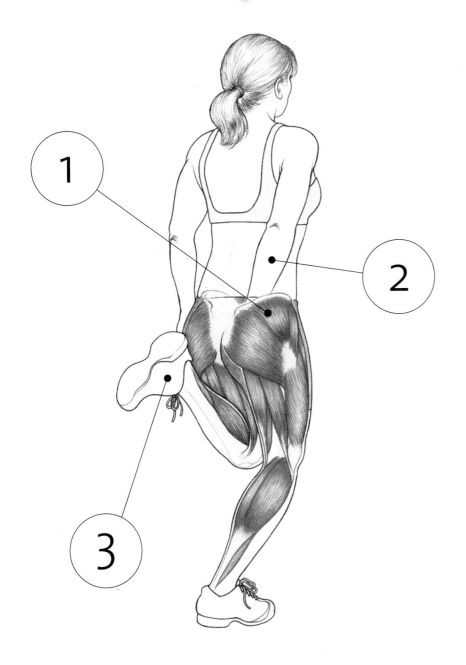

1 Stand tall, take the front of the foot (shoelaces), bring your heel into your backside and pull gently until you feel your quad pulling. For a deeper stretch push your working hip forward.

2 If you struggle with balance simply hold onto something with your other hand. Before races and training sessions hold each leg for 10-20 seconds, one time on each leg.

3 For a dynamic stretch, once your quads are warm, you can kick your heels into your backside 10-15 times without using your hands.

MUSCLES STRETCHED   *QUADS AND HIP FLEXES*

Stretches – calves

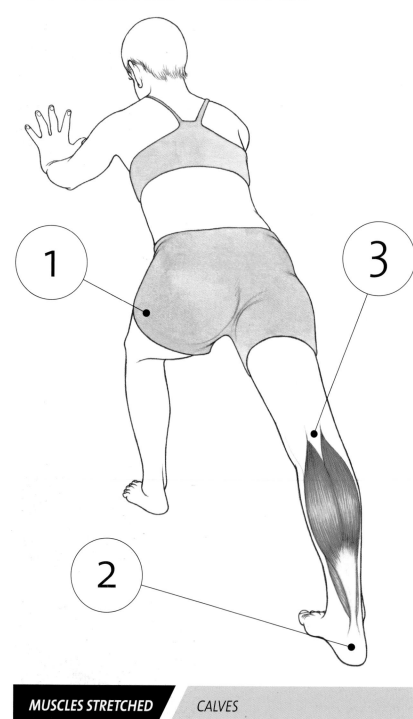

1 With your hands leaning against a wall, step one leg back keeping the leg straight and bending your front leg. Work the back heel into the floor.

2 To keep the stretch true make sure your weight is pressing forward and your back heel is lengthening.

3 To work the shorter muscle of the calf you can simply bend the back knee while still working the back heel down to the floor.

MUSCLES STRETCHED   *CALVES*

Stretches – child's pose

1 While kneeling down, sit back onto your heels and reach forward with your arms. You should have a dual stretch between sitting back and your hands reaching forward.

2 To increase the stretch down the side of your back, reach on the diagonal working your finger tips forward of the inside hand.

3 This stretch is great as the last thing you do in your workout. As well as stretching it is great for relaxing the body after a gruelling session.

MUSCLES STRETCHED *GLUTES, LOWER AND UPPER BACK*

cross
training
// STRONGER // TOUGHER
// MORE POWERFUL

The basics

If you are training for a particular sport there is no question that the best way to get fit for that purpose is to actually do that sport. If you want to be a runner then run, run and run some more, it's as simple as that.

So why cross train then?

Here we focus on four reasons to cross train: strengthening a weakness in a particular muscle or muscle group, injury prevention, motivation and ensuring that you maintain your general fitness. Most coaches will include a strength-training programme into an athlete's schedule whatever sport they are involved in. The amount of work that needs to be done in the gym can vary from sport to sport and, of course, the distance you are training for and the specific goals you have. Generally, the shorter events will require more power and strength, which can be gained with weights. For endurance events it is advisable that the strength training is done well away from the heavy mileage on the road or track. For example, if you are considering entering an event in six months, start your gym work with heavy weights and low reps (eight to 12 reps) for six to eight weeks, then lower the weights but increase the reps (maximum 15) for a couple of weeks. After this you can then

start to eliminate all weight work and concentrate on your running. However, everything depends on how serious and challenging your targets are. You can keep working on the strength training after these guidelines but be aware that your running could suffer as muscle fatigue may prevent you training properly for your main event. If you don't want to give up your cross training completely you could substitute this gym work for increased core work or specific stretching exercises. Overall, then, the benefits of spending time in the gym will be extra power in the legs, but don't overdo it – your training should also keep your core goals in mind.

Identify and strengthen weaknesses in the chain

One benefit of cross training is targeting a particular weakness in your body that is holding your running back. Once you have identified that weakness in your body while running or through analysis from a physio, you can head to the gym and really focus on that particular area, whether it's your legs or simply building up muscle groups for general body balance. So, for example, if you find some weakness in your hamstrings (back of the leg) and glutes (backside) while running you can use squats

(see page 84) and hamstring curls (see page 86) to strengthen these areas. By focussing on these muscles in the gym you really will notice a difference. However, it must still be remembered at all times that a lot of the pain we experience is due to the build up of lactic acid and the best way to combat this is to train in your chosen sport to keep the essential muscles for running in active use. You will get stronger from your running training, as muscle adaptations occur.

Injury prevention

Prevention of injury is probably the main reason to do specific training for your sport. Injuries can ruin months of hard work and for most non-sporting professionals, as well as ruining the sporting dream, this can make daily life very uncomfortable – just ask anyone with bad back pain they picked up in sport who has to sit in an office for eight hours a day. For example, if your hamstrings become very strong and tight and your opposite muscles (the quads) are weak then this can cause the pelvis to be held in a tilted alignment, which in turn causes poor back alignment and back pain. For these reasons, in the workout programmes outlined (see pages 109-111) you will find exercises which are not only geared towards running, but will also help keep a good

muscular balance in your body. When increasing your training workload you may experience discomfort in your body as muscles are asked to perform tasks at a much higher level to anything they have known before, although this discomfort often eases off over a long training period.

In the core section you will also find some Pilates exercises. These exercises are slightly modified for ease of use. However, if you can attend some Pilates or yoga classes these are an excellent way of keeping your core strong, maintaining an equal muscle balance and keeping your muscles supple. The added benefit of these exercises is that as these exercises are low impact there is reduced risk of injury and because of the low-energy output they can be done on your rest day. Stretching regularly also plays a key role in injury prevention and as this is more important for endurance runners than most sports, this aspect of your training should not be ignored (see Stretches on pages 69-77).

Motivation

Sometimes, when training for a specific event, you will just need a break from the routine of pounding the road. By having one day a week where you train your body in a different way you can really freshen up your mind as well. Many fast recreational runners will cycle or join in spin classes once a week. This will still give you cardiovascular benefits as well as changing the routine to give your running legs and mind a break. It can also be a good idea to add in some basic targets for your resistance training to keep motivated. You could, for instance, aim to increase your weight load by a certain percentage over a two-month period. Be aware that the targets you set will very much depend on where your starting point is. If you are already experienced in strength training your gains will be small because you will already have reached a decent level, so be realistic when setting your goals.

General fitness

Many people start on their running journey as a way of getting into shape and this is one of the greatest benefits of the sport. However, you must remember that if you just train in the sport you will only be fit for this sport. A certain amount of fitness will cross over to other fitness areas, but keeping yourself healthy and looking good often requires something a bit more specific. This can be seen clearly in different running distances. A good 100-metre runner will often struggle to do a good marathon time and vice-versa. So if one of your goals from running is good overall health you should not ignore cross training.

Legs – squats

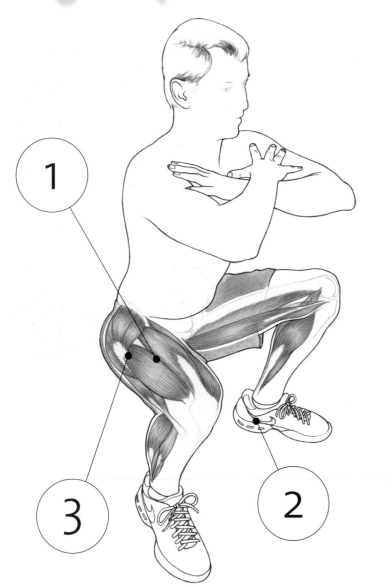

1 Keep knees soft and gently squeeze abs and bum. Tip your hips back as if you are sitting down in a chair, then go down until your upper leg is parallel with the floor. Push back up to the start position.

2 Keep all the weight driving through your heels, as this will maximize the workload in the glutes and hamstrings. Make sure your back stays long and keep knees over your middle toes.

3 As you start to fatigue, focus on keeping your abs and backside muscles engaged as this will protect the lower back. Use your breathing to help, releasing breath as you press up.

Muscles used

Primary: quads, glutes, hamstrings, lower back (erector spinae). Secondary: calves.

How will this help my running?

This exercise is all about strengthening the muscles you need for running, including the quads, hamstrings and lower back. The stronger your legs are the more you will be able to push off.

Legs – lunges

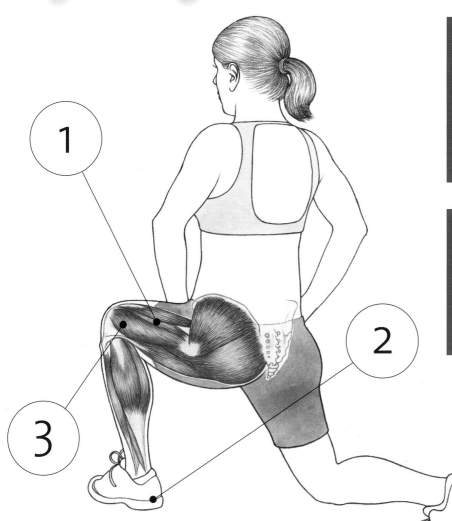

1 With feet hip-width apart keep knees soft and body tall, then take a long step back keeping back heel off the floor. Aim your back knee down to the floor and keep the front knee in line with your middle toe.

2 You need to keep your weight pressing through the front heel without allowing the front knee to travel forwards. Keep your pelvis gently tucked under your body.

3 The feel of the lunge movement is straight down and up. There should be no forward movement. This will keep the pressure on your front knee.

Muscles used

Primary: quads, glutes, hamstrings, calves.

How will this help my running?

This exercise promotes strength and power, enabling you to cover more distance on each stride. These type of power exercises also work the heart rate.

Legs – hamstring curls

1 Lie down on your front and place the back of your ankles on to the relevant pads and bend from the knees to lift the pads.

2 Make sure you use the full range of movement to work your hamstrings.
Note: although the exercise stays essentially the same there are different types of machines for this exercise.

3 Avoid allowing your hips to move up and down. Keep your hips still by pulling in your abs. This will also help you to avoid back injuries.

Muscles used

Primary:
hamstrings, glutes.

How will this help my running?

This isolation exercise focuses on the strength of the hamstring which you use as you land and as you kick your heel back.

Legs – leg extensions

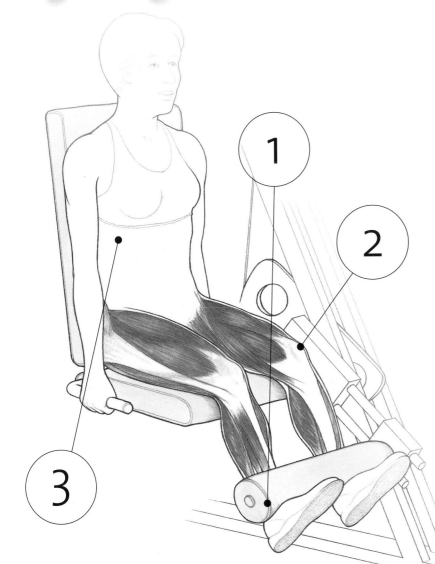

1 Sitting tall and to the back of the seat put your ankles underneath and in contact with the pads. Hold your hands lightly on the handles by your side.

2 Extend your legs fully, then allow them to bend back to your starting position. You should be in full control of the movement so don't kick your legs up or allow the weight to drop down.

3 Avoid using a weight that is too heavy as this will cause your backside to come off the seat when extending your legs.

Muscles used	How will this help my running?
Primary: quads.	Stronger quads will help you push off the ground harder, and also assist in softening your landings.

Legs – single leg squats

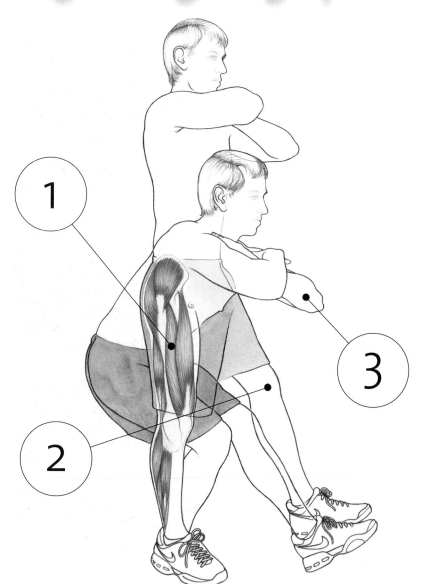

1 Standing on one leg have the other leg bent at a right angle with the knee at hip height. This is the position you will start and finish each rep.

2 Keeping the posture tall throughout the rep, bend your supporting knee sit back as if you are about to sit on to a chair.

3 This exercise is as much about balance as strength. So when starting you may want to use a wall as support. Lose this support as soon as possible to gain all the benefits.

Muscles used

Primary: glutes, quads, hamstrings, calves. Secondary: lower back.

How will this help my running?

Extra strength and stability of one leg, which is how we run. All the muscles of the legs you use to run will be working. This can also help create a better alignment when you run, so preventing pronation and supination.

Legs – jump squats

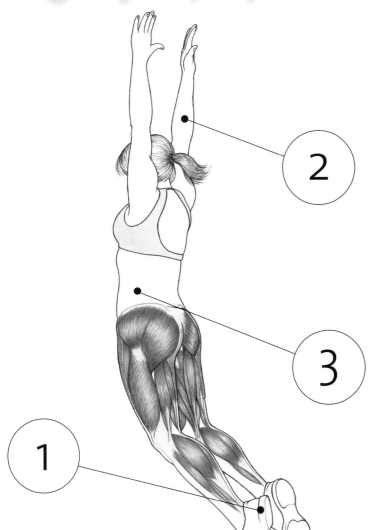

1 This is advanced dynamic work. Take a shallow squat, then jump forward pushing equally off both feet to jump as far as you can. Land through a heel-to-toe action and bend your knees on impact to cushion the landing.

2 Take a pause between each rep to steady your body so you are in a strong starting position. You can use your arms to gain momentum, using a natural swing.

3 As with all dynamic work there is a high risk of injury if the exercise is not performed correctly, so as you get tired make sure your abs are gently squeezed in and landings are soft. If you can't maintain this then it's time to stop.

Muscles used	How will this help my running?
Primary: quads, glutes, hamstrings, lower back. Secondary: calves.	Performing this exercise will give you the power your legs need to push off, and the control they need while landing. You will also feel your heart rate rising and working in your anaerobic zones.

Legs – single leg hops

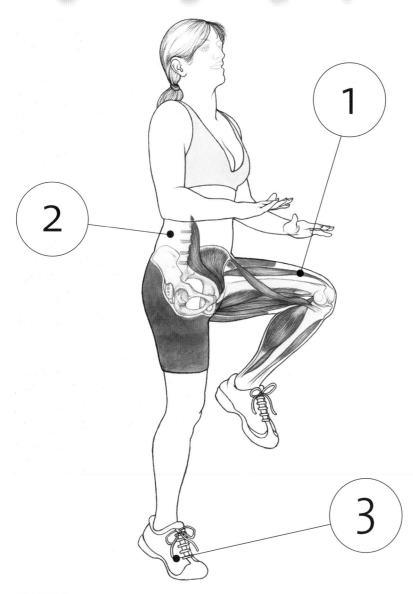

1 Just like the single leg squats, start standing on one leg and have the other leg bent at a right angle with the knee at hip height.

2 Hop as high as you can, making sure that you do not bend forward or lean back. You should try to land on the same spot as where you took off.

3 To prevent any damage to your back or knees, the landing in this exercise is crucial. Make sure you are cushioning your landings as if you are landing on a mattress.

Muscles used	How will this help my running?
Primary: glutes, quads, hamstrings, calves.	This is a great exercise to give you power when you push off your leg, control when landing on your leg and all the stability you will need when running.

Legs – squats on ball

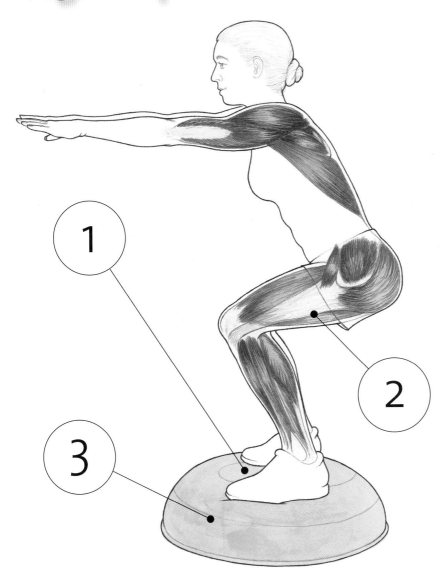

1 Start with your feet hip-width apart on the ball. Stand tall, then sit back and down keeping your back long and your chest lifted. Keep your knees in line with your middle toes.

2 All the weight needs to be going through the heel of your foot as this will take the pressure away from the knees and activate the glutes and hamstrings.

3 The action is the same as doing squats on the floor. You can also progress your lunges in a similar fashion by doing single leg squats.

Muscles used

Primary: quads, hamstrings, glutes, lower back. Secondary: calves, core.

How will this help my running?

As well as the strength benefits gained from the squat action, this exercise will help keep your posture tall when running, giving you a more efficient running action.

Legs – bench steps

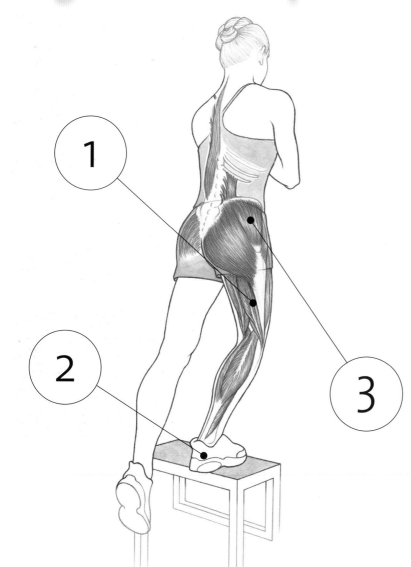

1 Stand about 30cm (about 12 inches) away from a step or bench. Step one foot up before bringing the other leg up, always keeping the foot and knee at a right angle.

2 When stepping onto the bench with your first leg, carefully put your heel down first. This will keep your body secure on the bench and activate the correct muscles.

3 Always keep your body straight and tall. The temptation is to lean forward from the hips. To increase the intensity you can hold weights in each hand.

Muscles used	How will this help my running?
Primary: quads, glutes. Secondary: hamstrings, calves.	This gives you strength and power in your quads, hamstrings and core, which will really help with some of the steeper hills when running.

Legs – calf raises

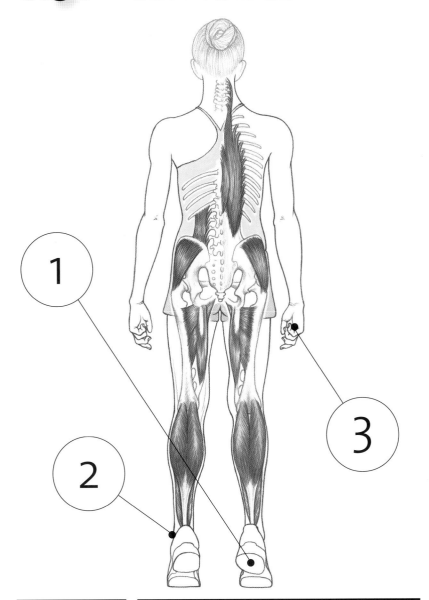

1 Keep feet hip-width apart and your body tall, then rise up high onto the balls of your feet, and lower back to starting position.

2 Keep your ankles in neutral alignment. The temptation is to let your heels fall out to the side. Always keep your whole body lifted and straight.

3 To increase the intensity you can hold a weight in each hand. If no equipment is available simply use cans of food or something heavy and easy to hold.

Muscles used	How will this help my running?
Primary: calves.	The calf muscles need to be really strong for runners. Every time your foot fully extends as you push off the floor your calf contracts.

Legs – lunges with one foot on ball

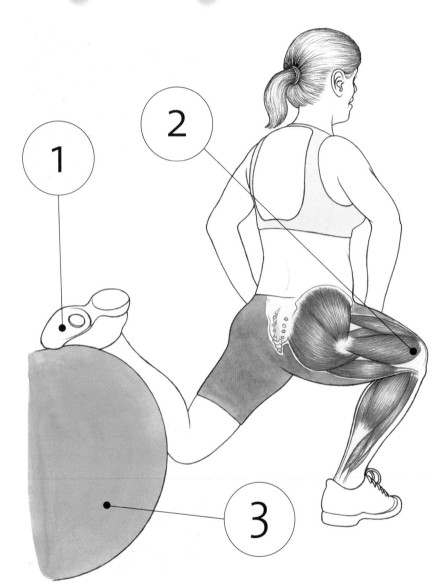

1 Have the top of one foot on the ball behind you. The weight should be on your front foot, which you should position as far forward as possible.

2 Bending the front leg make sure that your knee goes no further forward than your ankle. It should lower down to a 90-degree angle. Think of going straight up and down with all your weight pressing through the front heel.

3 This is an advanced exercise and requires strength and co-ordination. If you need the wall for support use it until you can manage without. If you don't have a exercise ball, you can use a more stable base such as a bench.

Muscles used	How will this help my running?
Primary: quads, glutes, hamstrings, calves.	This exercise will strengthen all the running muscles of the leg. It will force you to use one leg so you become equally strong in balance on both sides. Remember you use both legs to run.

Chest – press-ups

1 Start with your hands wider than your shoulders and then lower your chest down to the floor until there is a fist-size distance between your chest and the floor. Slowly push back to starting position.

2 Your body should remain in a straight line – pay particular attention to the shape of your back. Keep your hips in line and your chest coming down first as this will keep your body straight.

3 You can lower your knees down to lower the intensity of the press-up. You should also do this if you feel you are losing your body alignment.

Muscles used

Primary: pecs.
Secondary: triceps.

How will this help my running?

This exercise will help keep your posture tall, promoting that ideal running stance. It will also keep your body in good overall balance.

Back – bent-over rowing

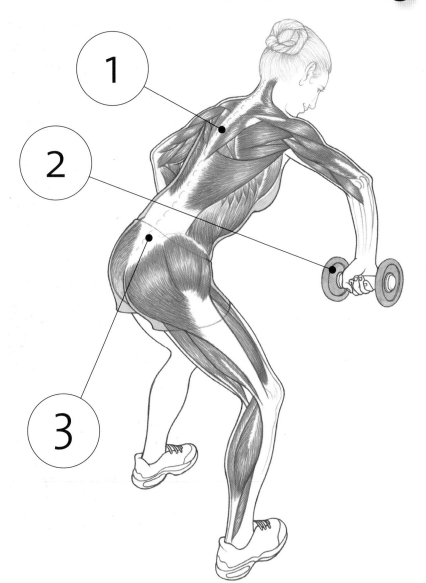

1 When lifting the weights feel your shoulder blades squeezing together. This will concentrate the workload in the centre of your back.

2 Start with the weights down by your knees. Stay in this bent-over position and squeeze the weights in towards the belly button in a rowing movement, before straightening your arms to the starting position again.

3 Staying in this position can be tough on your lower back and there is a temptation to curve your lower spine outwards. Avoid this by keeping your pelvis in the correct alignment and squeezing your abs.

Muscles used

Primary: neck, shoulder and back (trapezius). Secondary: biceps.

How will this help my running?

You will be working the centre of your back and lower shoulder muscles which help keep the posture open and stop the hunched posture often seen in runners.

* To do this exercise without weights, start in the same position but put both feet on a resistance band and pull round in an arc from your shoulders in the same path to the top as with weights.

Back – dead lift

1 Start with your heels under your hips, legs slightly bent, your back straight, hands just wider than your thighs and palms facing the body. Then lower the bar down to your knees by leaning forwards and concentrating on working your back. Pause briefly and come back to your starting point.

2 As you go through the reps keep your back long and do not allow any flexion or extension from your knees. Shoulders should be pulled back at all times.

3 All the weight should be in the heel of your foot and your knees soft without bending them. Avoid doing squats.

Muscles used	How will this help my running?
Primary: lower back, hamstrings, glutes.	This is a great exercise for gaining strength in the hamstrings, and will also protect the lower back as you gain strength there. Many runners complain of lower back pain.

Arms – bicep curls

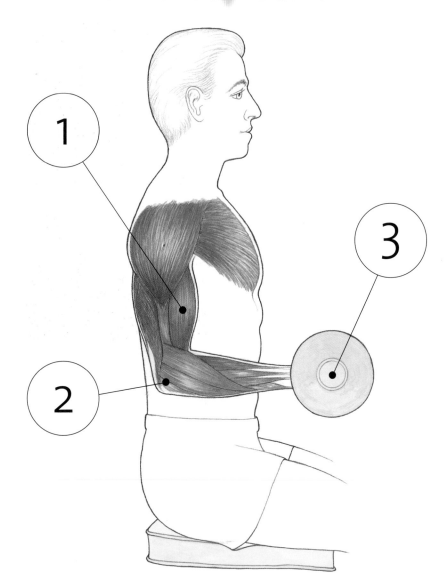

1 Hold the weights with your palms facing forwards while keeping your hands at a natural carrying grip. Bend at the elbow and curl the weights to your chest. Pause briefly then curl back to the horizontal starting position.

2 Keep your elbows close to your body and do not allow them to pull back behind the body alignment.

3 Your hands need to remain strong but soft. If you grip too hard you will feel your forearms work more as opposed to your biceps.

Muscles used	How will this help my running?
Primary: biceps.	Not specifically a running exercise, but will create balance in your body. For your 10 km runs you can use these muscles in conjunction with your shoulders to help pump the arms and create a bit more pace.

* To do this exercise without weights, start in the same position but put both feet on a resistance band and pull round in an arc from your shoulders in the same path to the top as with weights.

Arms – tricep dips

1 Start with your hands on a bench (or step) and positioned just wider than your thighs. Keep your backside close to the bench and, bending from the elbows, lower your body down and press back up.

2 Keep your shoulders pulled down all the time. At the bottom of the dip your elbows should go to a right angle and your wrists should stay in line.

3 You can make this exercise more intense by straightening your legs and flexing your feet. When doing this keep your backside close to the bench.

Muscles used

Primary: triceps.

How will this help my running?

Similar to the bicep curls, this will help create a good even strength to your body, but don't imagine that because you have big arms you will run better.

Shoulders – rotator cuff

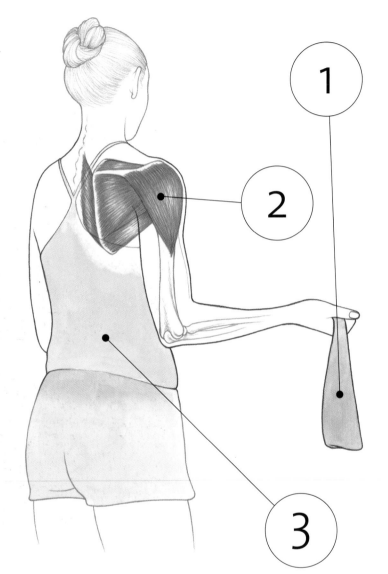

1 Using a resistance band, start with one end of the band tied to a pole and hold the other end in one hand. Ensuring you keep your working elbow close to your body pull your hand across the body at a right angle.

2 While keeping your elbow at a right angle, open your arm outwards from your body so you are squeezing the back of your shoulder.

3 This is a great exercise for keeping the shoulder alignment open. Make sure your posture stays true so you don't allow any movement around your back.

Muscles used	How will this help my running?
Primary: back of shoulder (rotator cuff).	Strong shoulders help to keep your upper body tall and avoids you hunching over, which is a common problem among longer distance runners.

Core – balance on one leg

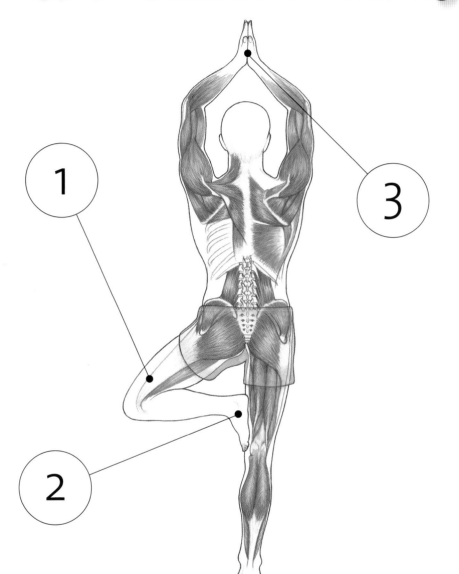

1 Standing tall, have your supporting leg straight, with your working leg lifted high above the knee cap, with the knee pointing out to the side.

2 Press your foot into your leg as this will help stabilize your body, but make sure you keep it away from your knee cap. Aim to keep your foot above your knee but if this is a struggle then calf height also works.

3 Place your hands in the prayer position, pushing the palms of the hands together. To de-stabilize and test the body further you can take your arms above your head or even close your eyes.

Muscles used	How will this help my running?
Primary: core Secondary: lower back, calves, quads.	Learning to balance will force you to engage your core muscles otherwise you have a good chance of falling over. This can help your body to engage your core muscles when running, thus protecting you from lower back pain.

Core – front plank

1

2

3

1 To get into position place your forearms flat on the floor with your elbows just behind your shoulder alignment. There should be a flat line between the crown of your head, hips and heels. Hold the position for 30 seconds or more.

2 Back alignment is crucial in this exercise. You must maintain the natural curve of your spine by keeping your pelvis centred. Pushing your weight back into your heels can really lengthen your spine.

3 If you cannot maintain the correct alignment, gently lower your knees to the floor. You should do this for a lower intensity option.

Muscles used

Primary: deep and superficial abs and lower back.

How will this help my running?

Core strength is essential for runners to ensure posture stays tall and straight, especially during long distances when tiredness kicks in.

Core – side plank

1 To get into position place one hand on the floor with your elbow in a direct line under your shoulder. Your hips should be stacked one on top of the other. Then lift up as if you a drawing away from a flame until your body is in position as per the illustration. Hold for 30 seconds or more.

2 As with the front plank the key is body alignment. Your back must maintain its natural curve – lengthen your legs as the will help to keep your back long.

3 A lower intensity alternative of this exercise is to bend your knees at a right angle so your feet are behind and lift up on your arm while balancing on your knees. This can be used if your shoulders are weak.

Muscles used

Primary: side abs, deep and superficial abs and lower back.

How will this help my running?

Strengthens your obliques and core muscles. Vital in helping to promote a good running posture and preventing back injury.

Core – sit-ups

1. Start with feet flat on the floor and your knees bent facing the ceiling. Lightly support your head with your hands but do not pull your neck. Using your abs, lift up your upper body so your shoulder blades come off the floor to about 45 degrees.

2. Lift up through your upper body and not from your neck. The key is getting the shoulder blades off the floor with your eye line looking through your knees at the highest point.

3. To get the best results keep pulling your belly button gently back towards the spine. For increased intensity and to improve balance, this exercise can be done with the base of your back balanced on an exercise ball.

Muscles used

Primary:
superficial abs.

How will this help my running?

Sit-ups will work your six-pack muscles, which are worked as you bring your legs through when running.

Core – shoulder bridge

1 Lie flat on your back with the soles of your feet on the floor and knees bent up to the ceiling. Slowly roll up through your pelvis then ease back to the starting position.

2 To increase the intensity you can hold the movement at the top then extend one leg up to the ceiling. Alternate legs.

3 At the top of the movement your shoulders, hips and knees should all be in a line. When rolling up and down, imagine your spine as a bicycle chain and roll through each link one at a time.

Muscles used

Primary: glutes, hamstrings, lower back, abs.

How will this help my running?

This exercise works all the smaller core muscles down the spine. You will be grateful for doing this exercise after those long training runs, as it will stop the back hurting.

Core – leg raises

1 Start on your back with your hands by your side. Lift up your legs and upper body at the same time so you create a 'V' shape with your body, then lower down.

2 The movement should be controlled and slow. Be very careful as you lower down to have full control of your body.

3 This is a tough exercise and performed incorrectly can cause injury to the back. A good option to start with is to keep the knees bent as you come up.

Muscles used

General: top of leg and abs, hip flexors.

How will this help my running?

This will work the hip flexors (top of the leg), and external abdominal muscles. Getting them stronger will help you bring your leg through more smoothly.

Core – back raises

1 Lie flat down with arms slightly away from your body with palms down but thumbs slightly turned up. Raise your upper body and legs off the floor.

2 Keep your abs gently pulled in and your bum muscles gently squeezed, as this will support the back. Movement up and down should be slow and controlled.

3 If you want more support for your back place your hands under your shoulders for support and push up from the floor. Use as much or as little pressure on the hands as you need.

Muscles used	How will this help my running?
Primary: lower back.	This exercise strengthens the lower back muscles to make sure that you can keep the posture true throughout your runs. Remember a good posture creates a more efficient and faster running action.

Core – hip abductor

1 Lying on you side, support your head with your hand. Have your bottom knee in front of your hips at a right angle. Keep top leg straight.

2 Flex your top foot, gently rotate your toes towards the floor so your heel is turning up towards the ceiling. Make sure the top leg is really lengthened.

3 Gently pulse the top leg up and down 10 times. Then create small circles one way 10 times and reverse and repeat the circle 10 times. Repeat this set two to three times.

Muscles used	How will this help my running?
Primary: glutes	This exercise really isolates the glute. This muscle is used in stabilizing the hips, which helps in the prevention of runners' knee.

Workout programme – beginners

Sets x2, reps x8-12 (sit-ups, core raises, back raises x15 reps), 1 min recovery between exercises.
Planks: aim for 30 second holds (reduce if losing technique).

To find your ideal weight for each exercise you should be able to complete the reps but just about hit failure on the final rep.
As a guide, the heaviest weight you would use would be for your larger muscle groups (eg glutes and quads used in squats)
and the lightest weight you would use would be for your smaller muscle groups (eg biceps in bicep curls).

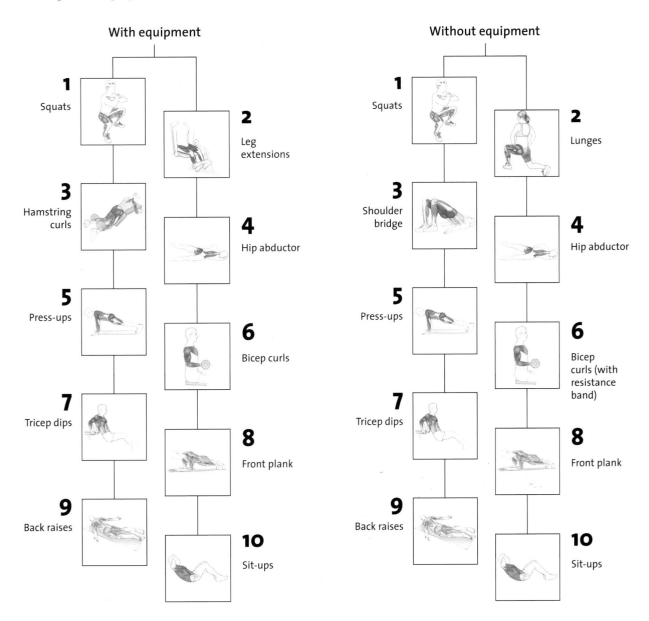

With equipment

1 Squats
2 Leg extensions
3 Hamstring curls
4 Hip abductor
5 Press-ups
6 Bicep curls
7 Tricep dips
8 Front plank
9 Back raises
10 Sit-ups

Without equipment

1 Squats
2 Lunges
3 Shoulder bridge
4 Hip abductor
5 Press-ups
6 Bicep curls (with resistance band)
7 Tricep dips
8 Front plank
9 Back raises
10 Sit-ups

Workout programme – intermediate

Sets x2, reps x10-15 (core raises x20 reps)

Planks: aim for 45 second holds (reduce if losing technique)

To find your ideal weight for each exercise you should be able to complete the reps but just about hit failure on the final rep. As a guide the heaviest weight you would use would be for your larger muscle groups (eg glutes and quads used in lunges) and the lightest weight you would use would be for your smaller muscle groups (eg shoulders in bent-over rowing).

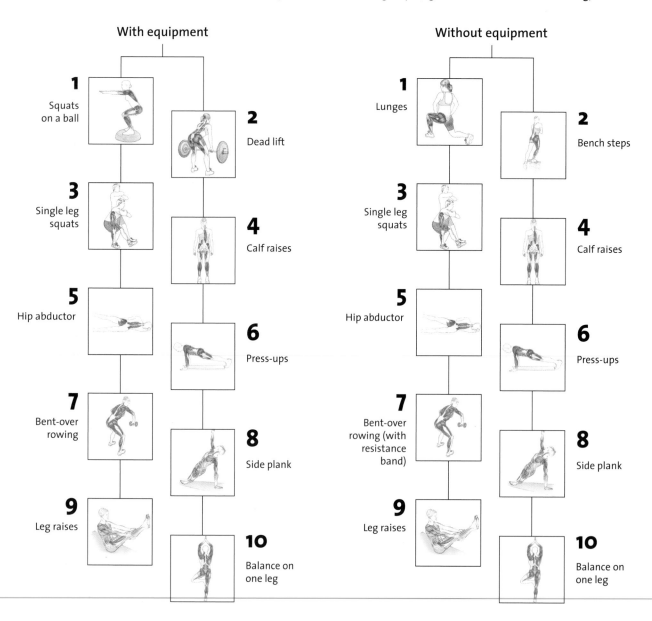

With equipment

1 Squats on a ball
2 Dead lift
3 Single leg squats
4 Calf raises
5 Hip abductor
6 Press-ups
7 Bent-over rowing
8 Side plank
9 Leg raises
10 Balance on one leg

Without equipment

1 Lunges
2 Bench steps
3 Single leg squats
4 Calf raises
5 Hip abductor
6 Press-ups
7 Bent-over rowing (with resistance band)
8 Side plank
9 Leg raises
10 Balance on one leg

Workout programme – advanced

Sets x3, reps x12-15 (core raises x30 reps)

Planks: aim for 1 min to 1 min and 30 seconds holds (reduce if losing technique)

To find your ideal weight for each exercise you should be able to complete the reps but just about hit failure on the final rep. As a guide, the heaviest weight you would use would be for your larger muscle groups (eg glutes and quads used in lunges) and the lightest weight you would use would be for your smaller muscle groups (eg shoulders in bent-over rowing).

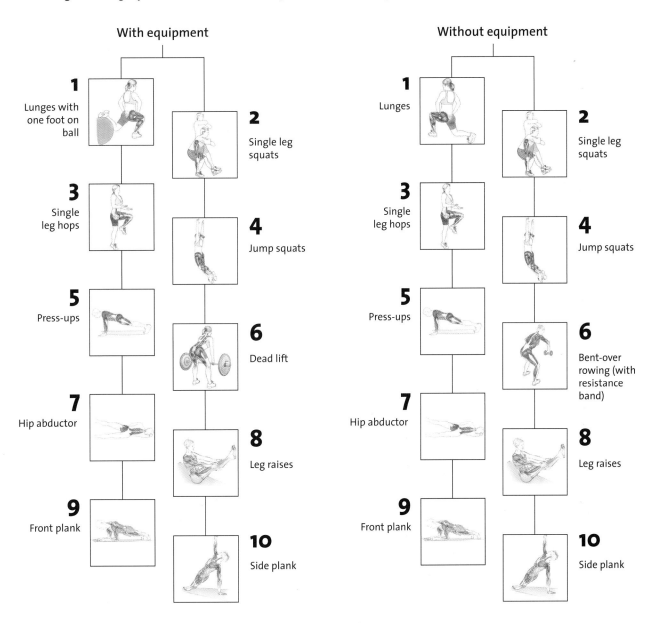

With equipment

1 Lunges with one foot on ball

2 Single leg squats

3 Single leg hops

4 Jump squats

5 Press-ups

6 Dead lift

7 Hip abductor

8 Leg raises

9 Front plank

10 Side plank

Without equipment

1 Lunges

2 Single leg squats

3 Single leg hops

4 Jump squats

5 Press-ups

6 Bent-over rowing (with resistance band)

7 Hip abductor

8 Leg raises

9 Front plank

10 Side plank

nutrition

// HEALTHIER // LIVELIER
// MORE ENERGETIC

The basics

Food and nutrition are the basic elements for a correct training regime in any sport. Think of your body as if it were a car – it could have the most powerful engine, the most aerodynamic shape or the best design but it would never run without its fuel. Food is the natural fuel for your body.

Food can be divided into four basic groups: **carbohydrates, proteins, fat** and **liquids** and each one of them is equally important in running our body, giving it energy, stamina, resistance and self-recovery. Each one of these elements is essential to our nutrition and is absolutely harmless to our health and body if taken in the right amounts, balanced in combination with all the others.

Carbohydrates are the fuel for your muscles. They provide the energy for your muscles to work.

Proteins build and repair muscles whenever they have been stressed during exercise.

Fats are energy stores for your body and help the correct functioning of the cells and maintaining your body's temperature.

Liquids maintain the right body fluid concentration and expel toxins.

A correct combination of each one of the above-mentioned elements, adjusted depending on the sport and your body's response, will provide you with the correct nutrition needed, both for training and competition.

A basic diet for an athlete or an active person (someone who trains three times a week for more that 60 minutes per training session) should amount to a daily intake of 3,000–4,500 calories per day, according to the sport and the amount of training. This might seem a lot more than what you heard in your sports club or while chatting while jogging but remember that this diet is not planned in order to make you lose weight but to give you an understanding of what your body needs to perform at its best while under the athletic stress.

If you eat the right foods at the right time, plan your weekly diet with the same care you use to plan your training, weight will never be a problem and you will understand how a correct diet (as a plan to correctly feed your body, instead of a rush into weight loss) will drastically improve your life as well as your athletic performance

Nutrition in sports is as important as the exercise. Again, your body, as a car, needs the right fuel to perform at its best.

There are four key steps you need to understand before planning your diet:

1. Do not get too hungry as it will make you take the wrong dietary choices and swallow whatever you can find. Have at least five meals a day, calibrating the amounts at each meal.

2. Eat at least three different kinds of foods at each meal as mono-eating will make your body incapable of digesting correctly what you don't usually eat. Choosing different kinds of vegetables, fish and meat, will provide your body with different vitamins and minerals.

3. Always balance the food elements at each meal. Every meal should be based on carbohydrates combined with proteins and fats (amounts change from person to person; but a good starting base is a balance of 50 per cent carbohydrates, 30 per cent proteins and 20 per cent fats).

4. Try to choose foods in their natural state. A banana is better than an energy bar and an orange is better than orange juice for instance.

Assess your diet

People tend to be obsessed by their body shape. It is a normal feeling given the kind of images the media world sends us every day. When you assess your ideal diet, try to forget about your shape and think realistically for a moment about what goals you want to achieve athletically. By doing so you will be more focused on understanding, planning and applying the correct diet to everyday life.

First question: do you have breakfast?

Eat breakfast every morning. If you train early in the morning try to wake up half-an-hour before you normally would just to make sure you eat a good amount of food for breakfast. If waking up earlier is going to be impossible, try to eat more carbohydrates the night before, and top up the next morning with some snack. It's very important for you to eat something one hour before training, as it will guarantee the sugars flow in your blood, while the muscles will use the energy stored during the night.

Avoid hyper-protein breakfasts. Remember that every meal should be based around carbohydrates. A little sample of ideal food for breakfast would be:

- Porridge with cottage cheese or ricotta cheese and some nuts.
- A cup of milk or yoghurt over a bowl of cereals with a banana and some raisins. Remember that all-bran cereals tend to be stressful for the bowels, which is inappropriate for training and competition. Also avoid sugar-coated cereals.
- A sandwich made with two slices of whole-grain bread and 60 grams of smoked salmon (you could add a some light cream cheese) and an orange or a glass of orange juice.
- Muesli with yoghurt and one piece of fruit.

If you feel the need for a boost of caffeine, feel free to drink it, as it would not interfere with your training (although it gives stomach acidity to some people). No person is the same, which means it's up to you to find your right intake by calibrating and testing day after day to find the right proportions and taste to suit you.

Second question: do you snack after training?

Remember that eating and drinking after training is the only way you can start to refuel your empty muscles. You can choose what kind of snack you should have, depending on the amount of energy spent and the length of the interval before your next training session. This is the moment where you really train your muscles to intake and store more and more glycogen.

You have two options: either you go for a low or a high GI snack. GI is the acronym for Glycemic Index which is a measure of the effects of carbohydrates on sugar levels. Carbohydrates can be released into the blood slowly (in that case they have a low GI) or quickly (high GI). Although important for the control of illnesses like diabetes, the control of the GI is something that most athletes don't really worry about. What you must decide is the kind of recovery you want from your diet.

If you have two training sessions in one day, or another training session the morning after, then you might want to consider a high GI recovery, choosing food like corn flakes, white bread, watermelon or baked potatoes. On the other hand, it's been shown that a low or medium GI recovery, because of its slower release of sugars, will be more effective in the long run, using food like fruits, vegetables, whole-grain breads, pasta, milk and yoghurt.

Remember that gulping down gallons of protein shakes after training will be almost useless.

You need mainly carbohydrates to refuel your muscles and only some proteins to recover the stressed muscles and help new ones to grow.

Third question: do you ever go hungry during the day?
If you do sometimes go hungry in the day you need adjust your plans to make sure this doesn't happen. Make sure you plan your meals and snacks beforehand by experimenting with your meals for a few days and organize your day around the food you know you will need.

Ideally you should have one substantial breakfast before leaving your house, one snack no longer than four hours after breakfast (between 10.00 and 11.00 for most people), one lunch (if you think it would be better then prepare it the night before, in order to avoid rushing into eating any food you find in the shops when hungry). Then have another snack three to four hours later, a good dinner (try to avoid pasta, rice and bread for dinner, unless preparing for a competition or the night before the competition itself) and one last evening snack.

Fourth question: do you find yourself fatigued during training?
There could be different reasons for being fatigued during training.

- A low glycogen storage. The glycogen has been burned and you are now using your proteins and fats as fuel, provoking your blood to carry ketones to your brain. In this case you should eat more carbohydrates before training and more carbohydrates after training, in order to teach your muscles to store as much glycogen as possible.
- Dehydration. A lack of liquids means your body can't cool down properly, endangering the health of your cells and making the expulsion of carbon dioxide and lactic acid more difficult.

Carbohydrates

One of the many myths you may have read is that carbohydrates are fattening. This is untrue. Fats are fattening, carbohydrates are the basic fuel you need to eat in order to have enough energy in your muscles. In a sports diet carbohydrates are an absolute must of your nutrition requirements.

Carbohydrates can be divided into two groups: simple and complex. Simple carbohydrates are monosaccharides (single-sugar molecules: fructose, glucose and galactose) and disaccharides (double-sugar molecules: table sugar, milk sugar, honey and refined syrups). Fruits and vegetables contain many different kinds of carbohydrates, which is one of the reasons why your diet should include a good variety of vegetables and fruits.

During digestion your stomach turns the sugars and carbohydrates into glucose, before the latter is then turned into a polymer (a chain of five or more sugar molecules) called glycogen. Glycogen is the key to your energy levels. Glycogen gets stored in your muscles and your liver, supplying your body with the right amount of energy for your training or your competition.

While the glycogen stored in your muscles will function as an energy reserve to move your body and train your muscles, the one stored in your liver will provide a slow-release of sugars into your bloodstream, guaranteeing a constant amount of sugars to your brain. This is important, because the sugars in your brain will influence your performance drastically.

Did you ever hear about, or ever hit the infamous 'wall'? The wall is something many professional athletes have hit during their career. It's a moment during which you become sure you are not going to make it to the finish. The wall is not a metaphysical concept, it is simply the moment when you have no more sugars flowing to your brain. Having the right amount of glycogen stored in both your muscles and your liver will help you avoid the wall.

What is the main difference between the different sugars, then? While refined sugars, soft drinks and energy drinks will only provide an energy supply, vegetables and fruits will supply, along with different amounts of glucose, also vitamins and minerals which will help spark and run your body engine in the correct way.

Always try to eat foods in their natural state. Whole-wheat breads, brown rice, brown pasta, as all the nutritional elements you will find in unrefined products, are more valuable than the ones you will find in refined ones. The same concept can be applied to cooked carbohydrates – it is preferable to undercook vegetables, in order for them to retain the vitamins and minerals contained in them along with the sugars and starches. This leads to a very important point you should be aware of. Your muscles need to be trained not only through exercise, but also by making them capable of storing the biggest amount of glycogen possible. How do you do that? By eating the right carbohydrates in the right amount.

During training you put your muscles under stress in order to grow them and make them stronger. At the same time, by supplying them with the right amount of carbohydrates, you will teach them to store more glycogen.

In 100 grams of untrained muscle you can store only 13 grams of glycogen but the same amount of trained muscle will store about 32 grams, while a muscle trained to be loaded with carbohydrates will be able to store between 35 and 40 grams. Needless to say, the latter is the muscle that will perform better and for longer.

Carbohydrates

1 Unrefined foods will have a better nutritional value than the refined ones. Wild rice, whole-wheat breads, brown pasta, popcorn (unbuttered), oats and porridge, raw fruits and vegetables, etc.

2 Always make sure that any meal you take during the day is based around carbohydrates. Try to think in terms of the proportions stated above (50-30-20).

3 Vary your food as much as possible. A good way is to plan your meals by colour (green leaves or broccoli, tomatoes, peppers, carrots, oranges, apples, blueberries, etc).

4 Always make sure that before and after training you have the right amount of carbohydrates to restore your energy levels and sugars in your bloodstream. Once the glycogen is used up your body will start burning your fat as an energy supplement. Although this is the basic concept of how to trim down your stomach, bear in mind that such a process is detrimental to your performance, as your bloodstream will carry ketons to your brain instead of sugars, amplifying your tiredness and affecting your mood.

Proteins

Let's start by refuting another myth: proteins do not make you stronger, exercise does. There is always a magic aura around words such as proteins and amino acids, believed to be the mysterious ingredients to a muscular body. Don't worry, it's not so mysterious.

Proteins have many different roles in your body. They help build new muscles, repair those stressed by exercise, are the reason your hair and nails grow, energize your immune system and, above all, help replace red blood cells. A protein-based diet is useless. Drinking protein shakes, eating too many egg whites, or stuffing yourself with chicken breast will lead to poor results. An over-intake of proteins can be useless, even counterproductive. Your body can store only a certain amount of protein or amino acids and if you exceed this they will be either burned for energy (a scarce amount if compared to carbohydrates) when the body runs out, or stored as glycogen or fat. There are two main problems you can face if following a diet with too much protein.

1. It will prevent you from eating the right amount of carbohydrates, lowering the amount of energy stored in your muscles.
2. It will break down into urea, an organic compound your body eliminates through urine. People who eat too many proteins will need to increase their fluid intake to eliminate as much urea as possible, leading to frequent visits to the toilet.

By eating too many proteins you also increase the chance of eating excessive fats (through meats and condiments) that your body will store. The correct amount of protein an athlete can digest varies but as a rule of thumb, is calculated to be between 1.2 and 1.6 grams per body weight kilogram per day. That is usually less than your daily intake by only eating meat, fish, dairy products or legumes. The ideal intake would be a daily total of about 150g to 200g, adding the proteins you should get from two servings of low-fat dairy products (milk, yoghurt and cheese) per day.

Meats can be divided into three kinds: white meats, red meats and fish. An ideal sports diet should include all kinds of meats in your weekly plan.
- Fish is the best option as the fats it contains are unsaturated (including the famous Omega-3), so is a better choice than the saturated fats commonly found in meats and dairy products.
- White meat is preferable to red meat as it usually contains less fat (if it is either breast or properly skinned thigh and drumsticks).
- Lean red meat, although not the healthiest option, should be eaten between three and four times per week. Red meat contains iron and zinc and iron is an essential part of haemoglobin, a protein that transports oxygen to your muscles and brain. If you are missing the right amount of iron you could suffer fatigue and exhaustion. Zinc is a mineral that plays a big role in removing carbon dioxide from your muscles when you are exercising. A good red meat is venison as it contains a lower quantity of saturated fat.

With dairy products, you should eat low-fat. Semi-skimmed milk and yoghurt are close to the ideal intake percentage (they contain a percentage of 40 per cent carbohydrates, 35 per cent proteins, 25 per cent fat), so are a perfect snack. It's an easy way to eat proteins and also supply vitamin D and calcium and the right amount of potassium, phosphorus and riboflavin. Potassium and phosphorus help your body in metabolizing the calcium to strengthen your bones, while riboflavin is a vitamin that helps your body to transform the food into energy.

Proteins

1 Choose fish before white meat or red meat, but make sure you eat all three kinds during the week.

2 Include proteins in every meal.

3 You can find all the proteins you need in the food you eat – you don't need to use shakes, bars or pills.

4 Try to eat low-fat dairy products at least once, preferably twice a day.

5 Do not overfeed yourself with proteins, as it is useless.

Fats

Fat is as important in your diet as any other food element. Fat helps provide the temperature regulation of your body, helps the health of skin and hair and provides a safety coating for your internal organs.

The most important thing is to know what kinds of fat you should eat and in what quantities. Fats can be divided into hard fats and soft fats. Hard fats are the fats that come in the form of meat lard, chicken skin or butter, while soft fats, the ones you should favour in your diet, are in the form of olive oil and canola oil.

As mentioned earlier, calories from fat should correspond to about 20 per cent of your diet. The most important thing to remember is to stay away from Hydrogenated Trans Fats, which are a very unhealthy result of a chemical process that adds hydrogen to both mono and polyunsaturated fats.

Don't be afraid of eating fats during your resting periods. Many people think if you don't exercise your muscles will turn into fat and you will gain weight. That is untrue. Muscles and fat are two distinct components of your body and you will only gain weight by taking more calories from fat than the ones you are burning, which, in the doses that have been mentioned before, is very unlikely.

You might have seen people in the gym torturing their abs, hoping to lose their belly by over-exercising the part closest to it. What you need to understand is that you lose your excessive fat by exercising the whole body and consuming the calories that you have taken. Let's put it this way: if you want to lose fat, you need to grow your muscles (in the whole body), as bigger muscles consume more calories. Don't try to over-stress specific areas of your body, as this is useless.

Remember that fats are what give taste to your food, helping to make it more favourable to your palate. As you are making an effort to stick to a dietary plan for your athletic training, try to enjoy it as much as possible, adding the right amount of healthy fats to your meals.

Fats

1 Olive oil is a monounsaturated fat and is the best choice. Always try to buy extra-virgin olive oil and use it to cook and dress any food you want. The ideal amount should be around two teaspoons for each meal.

2 Nuts – like walnuts, almonds, pistachios, macadamia, Brazilian nuts, pine kernels, olives – are also a good choice for fat intake. Each one of them is a different size and contains a different amount of fat, so it's important to weigh them so you know approximately how many you need. For example: cashew nuts, peanuts, almonds, pine kernels, require a dose of nine grams per meal while walnuts, macadamias, hazelnuts, pecans and pistachios are about seven to eight grams per meal. For avocado and green olives allow a bit more (about 18 grams for the avocado and 30 grams for the olives).

3 Fish oil is another good choice, as it is rich in healthy fats. However, not many people like the taste and it would be a pity to waste a whole meal because of it.

Liquids

Water is the base of life. Your body is made in the most part by liquids and any loss of liquids has to be quickly restored.

Water does the following.

- It keeps your blood liquid, helping the correct transportation of oxygen, glucose and fat, while taking away carbon dioxide and lactic acid.
- It helps keep your body cool by absorbing heat from your muscles, sweating the heat out, cooling the skin through evaporating sweat and allowing the cooled down epidermis to cool the blood that cools down the organs. It's a positive vicious cycle.

Thirst is the most common sensation our body delivers to make us aware that we need to restore our balance. This sensation becomes more complicated when we deal with sports however.

There are many variables to be taken into consideration when you are exercising. There is the level of preparation, the weather, the fact your mind is focused on a goal, your body is too well trained or, because of the water on your body, you don't feel the heat. Bear in mind that, while exercising, your brain will communicate 'thirst' to you when you have already lost about one per cent of liquids and then it might be too late to rehydrate yourself. At that point your heart is beating more than needed, burning more glycogen than it should. At a two per cent loss you are officially dehydrated and at three per cent your body could be impaired in continuing the task.

The secret is to plan your drinking as well as your eating. Evaluate the amount of liquids you lose during a training session. To do so, weigh yourself naked before the training and right after, before drinking. The difference in weight will tell you the amount of liquids you lost. Your urine should always be a pale yellow; if it is dark and dense it means that there are too many metabolic wastes compared to the amount of water.

It takes between eight and 12 hours before your body becomes fully rehydrated so always plan your drinking during both your everyday life and training. By sweating you not only lose liquids but also electrolytes such as magnesium, potassium, sodium and calcium.

Always start your training session fully rehydrated from the session before by drinking between five and eight millilitres per kilo of your body weight. You can add sodium to your drink or chose a sodium enhanced drink, as it might help retain the water in your body.

You can use sodium in food and beverages after your training if you need to rehydrate quickly for a second session (up to 12 hours after the first one). Drinking between 30 per cent and 50 per cent more fluids than the ones you lost during exercise should be enough to re-establish the right concentration of liquids in your body.

Try to stay away from alcohol as much as possible. It causes strong dehydration as it is a potent diuretic and it would make you waste more liquids than you should. Also remember alcohol is a depressant and it suppresses drastically your motor skills along with your mood.

Pre- and post-competition planning

Before the competition

Your pre-competition training should be winding down (tapering) in the few days before the event (see Training Programmes page 149). This is because your muscles need time to recover from hard exercise. During this time, while you are reducing your training load you should be re-establishing the glycogen in your muscles, rehydrating yourself and mending the stressed muscles by eating some proteins.

Try to interpret your pre-competition training as a final rehearsal for the real event. Some people think that stuffing themselves with pasta the night before the competition will be enough but things are a bit more complicated than that.

During training you will have taught your muscles to store a good amount of glycogen in order to have a good reserve in every training session. The more you train your muscles with exercise, the more glycogen your muscles will be able to store, if educated to receive it.

From one or two weeks before your competition you should slowly increase the amount of carbohydrates by about 100 grams per day. The day before the competition

itself you should start loading your body with carbohydrates from breakfast time.

Every athlete reacts differently to a competition. Some have no problem having a good dinner the night before – others find it difficult to digest food because of the excitement or worry. Therefore, start eating carbohydrates from the beginning of the day.

If you feel like eating dinner try to vary the type of carbohydrates as much as you can. Pasta by itself might do the trick, but remember that fruits and vegetables contain slow sugar-releasing carbohydrates and they will help for endurance the day after. Avoid bran flakes or anything that you know could lead to stomach problems.

Every sport has its pros and cons when it comes to taking on liquid. Cyclists will crow that they can always carry their liquids with them and never need to waste time, while for swimmers, once the event has started, that's it for liquid intake. Runners are somewhere in-between these two examples. In well-organized races it is rarely necessary to carry any liquid as these will be provided at regular refreshment stations along the way. However, it is always worth checking

beforehand just how frequent these stops are and what type of liquid is on offer. Rather carry a bottle of drink than go short on your regular intake of liquid (or your preferred drink) during a run.

Training brings a different dimension and you may be happy to carry what you need for your run. There are alternatives to being a pack horse, however such as planning your route via places you know have water taps or shops where you can buy a drink (don't get caught up worrying about the few seconds it takes to buy a drink). Another alternative is the drive the route before your run and drop your drinks at regular intervals en route behind bushes or walls and then simply stop and pick them up on your run.

On the morning of the competition, according to the time the event starts, there are few rules you need to follow.

- Make sure you wake up in the morning with the right fluid balance. You can easily determine it by the colour of your urine.

- Start by having a big glass of water and breakfast or, if the competition is too early to have breakfast, make sure you load some more carbohydrates one

hour before the event. This will make sure that your liver will produce enough sugar to be delivered to your brain throughout the duration of the competition.

- Drink your water between one to two hours before the race so you can expel it before the race starts.

After the competition

As you will have seen, after the event you need to let your body recover by rebalancing the glycogen and the fluids. Take advantage of the first hour after the event, as it will be the period when you body will assimilate all the nutrients best.

Carbohydrates mixed with a little protein is the best option to have both glycogen delivered to your muscles while reducing the emission of cortisol, the hormone that breaks down your muscles during exercise.

According to whether you will have a short or a long time before the next competition, you will have to find the right way to fully recover your muscles and blood.

Different athletes prefer different solutions according to their experience. The main thing is to plan a good nutrition schedule. If you know you have to compete in a number of competitions that are close together, you might want to plan your diet starting from the week before, in such way that it will be faster to recover between the events.

If you have two events back to back you want to make sure you will recover immediately after the first one by over-loading yourself with high-GI carbohydrates and liquids that will restore not only the fluids but also the electrolytes (some sport drinks do that). Try to drink as much as possible and judge the level of rehydration from the colour of your urine and comparing your weight before and after the event. If you happen to have more than two competitions in a span of more than two days, keep in mind that slow-GI carbohydrates have been proven to be more effective in the long run.

If you have enough time to recover after the event (one week), make sure you rebalance your fluids and have a little snack combining carbo-hydrates and proteins in the usual balance and then take your time, by simply starting the nutritional plan where you left it before the prepa-ration to the competition.

Recipes

OATS, RICOTTA AND PISTACHIOS

Ingredients
- *50 grams rolled oats*
- *140 grams of ricotta cheese*
- *8-10 pistachios, no shells*
- *Pinch of salt or honey*

Preparation Boil the oats in water until reaching your preferred consistency. In a bowl, mix the cooked oats, the ricotta cheese and pistachios. Add either a pinch of salt or half teaspoon of honey, depending on whether you prefer savoury or sweet. This is a perfect balanced snack, which combines proteins, carbohydrates and fat.

COTTAGE CHEESE WITH WARM BLUEBERRIES AND WALNUTS

Ingredients
- *220 grams of blueberries*
- *1 teaspoon of fructose*
- *70 grams of low-fat cottage cheese*
- *3 walnuts*

Preparation Warm the blueberries in a saucepan over low heat with fructose and a little bit of water and keep stirring gently until the berries are softened. Place the cottage cheese in a bowl and pour the fruits over it. Sprinkle with the crumbled walnuts. Perfect as a snack.

STUFFED SQUID

Ingredients
- *1 big squid (200 grams cleaned – keep the tentacles)*
- *2 teaspoons of chopped parsley and a little chopped garlic*
- *250 grams of grated fresh whole-grain bread or whole-grain breadcrumbs*
- *30 grams of grated Parmesan cheese*
- *1 tablespoon of olive oil*

Preparation Keep the squid body intact. For the filling: chop the tentacles and add them to a bowl along with the parsley, garlic, fresh breadcrumbs and Parmesan. Start pounding the mixture with your hands and add water and oil as needed. Fill the squid with the mix and close it with a toothpick. Put it in the oven for 30 minutes, using any leftover paste to coat the squid. Serve with a side of salad or a piece of fruit cut up.

BUTTER-FREE EGGS FLORENTINE

Ingredients
- 300 grams of spinach
- White wine vinegar
- 35 grams of cottage cheese
- 2 slices of whole-grain bread, toasted
- 2 eggs, poached
- Salt and pepper to taste
- Grated Parmesan cheese or shredded mild Cheddar cheese

Preparation Boil spinach until lightly soft. Mix a teaspoon of vinegar to the cottage cheese and mix well. Place spinach over the two slices of toasted bread. Arrange cooked, drained eggs over the top of the spinach then pour the cottage cheese over the eggs. Sprinkle with salt, pepper and grated Parmesan cheese.

SPICY OATS WITH GRILLED CHICKEN BREAST (OR VENISON STEAK)

Ingredients
- 3 teaspoons olive oil
- 1/2 red onion
- Pinch of chilli powder, pinch of paprika, 1 bay leaf
- 1 garlic clove
- 350 grams of raw oats (in grains)
- Grilled chicken breast or 120 gram venison steak
- Parsley

Preparation Mix olive oil and 3 tablespoons of water in a cooking pan. Chop up the onion and cook it in the oily water adding chilli powder, paprika, the bay leaf and garlic until golden. Add oats and let them roast a bit. Then add water and let them cook for 30 minutes. While it's cooking grill the chicken breast or venison steak. Serve with a sprinkle of chopped parsley.

FRESH SALAD

Ingredients
- *300 grams of cherry tomatoes*
- *300 grams of cucumber*
- *1/4 red onion, softened in warm water and a teaspoon of vinegar*
- *300 grams of low-fat Greek yoghurt*
- *2 teaspoons olive oil*
- *Salt and pepper to taste*
- *Pinch chives and dill*
- *Paprika to taste*

Preparation Cut the cherry tomatoes in half and the cucumbers into cubes. Mix the cherry tomatoes, cucumber, onion and Greek yogurt in a salad bowl. Add olive oil, salt and pepper, and sprinkle with chives, dill and paprika according to taste. Perfect and easy to make.

VENISON STEW

Ingredients
- *140 grams diced venison*
- *Salt and black pepper to taste*
- *1 tablespoon chopped fresh thyme*
- *3 tablespoons olive oil*
- *1 chopped onion*
- *300 grams chopped celery*
- *120 grams chopped carrots*
- *1 tablespoon chopped garlic*
- *200 grams chopped tomatoes*
- *150 grams chopped red peppers*
- *2 bay leaves*
- *1 glass red wine*
- *1 slice whole-grain bread, toasted*

Preparation In a mixing bowl, toss the venison with salt and black pepper, half the thyme and a little sprinkle of oil. In a large pot, over a high heat, add the rest of the olive oil. When the oil is hot, sear the meat for 2 to 3 minutes, stirring occasionally. Add the onions and let them cook for 4 minutes. Add the celery and carrots. Season with salt and pepper. Sauté for 4 minutes. Add the garlic, tomatoes, red peppers, the rest of the thyme, and bay leaves to pan. When the water from the vegetables is evaporated add the red wine. Add some boiling water if needed. Bring the liquid up to a boil, cover and reduce to a simmer. Simmer the stew for 45 minutes to 1 hour, or until the meat is very tender. If the liquid evaporates too much add a little more. Serve on a shallow bowl over a slice of whole-grain toasted bread.

LEMON SOLE WITH FENNEL AND ORANGE SALAD

Ingredients
- 1 pinch sea salt
- 1 pinch smoked paprika
- 1 pinch ground cinnamon
- Dill
- 2 teaspoons of olive oil
- 1 lemon sole (200 grams)

For the fennel and orange salad
2 bulbs fennel, thinly sliced
1/2 red onion, finely sliced
6 black olives, thinly sliced
1 orange, sliced and then cut into quarters
2 teaspoons of olive oil

Preparation Preheat the oven to 190°C (370°F)/gas 5. Mix together sea salt, smoked paprika, cinnamon and dill. Coat the lemon sole in the spice mixture. Lightly grease a cooking foil sheet with a little olive oil and place in a baking tray. Place the sole on the foil and then close the foil, joining the sides together. Let the fish cook for 10-12 minutes according to taste. Meanwhile, prepare the salad. Place the salad ingredients in a bowl and toss. Serve the fish on top of the salad and drizzle over the remaining olive oil.

GREEK SALAD

Ingredients
- 100 grams of Romaine lettuce
- 1/2 red onion, tendered in warm water
- 6 black olives
- 200 grams of tomatoes
- 200 grams of cucumber
- 90 grams of feta cheese
- 2 teaspoons of olive oil
- Oregano or basil
- 1/2 squeezed lemon
- Salt and black pepper according to taste

Preparation Cut all the ingredients into cubes, except for the onion, which should be thinly sliced. In a large salad bowl, combine the Romaine lettuce, onion, black olives, tomatoes, cucumber and feta cheese. Whisk together the olive oil, oregano/basil, lemon juice, salt and black pepper. Toss and serve.

SPAGHETTI BOLOGNESE

Ingredients
- 2 tablespoons olive oil
- 1/2 white onion, chopped
- 1 carrot, chopped
- 2 celery legs, chopped
- 75 grams of lean mincemeat
- 1 glass of red wine
- 400 grams of tomatoes
- 100 grams of brown spaghetti
- Parmesan cheese, grated

Preparation In a large saucepan mix olive oil and two tablespoons of water. Over medium heat cook the onion until soft and brown. Stir in carrot and celery and cook until tender. When the vegetables are cooked, increase heat to medium heat, add meat and cook for 4 minutes until it has barely browned, tossing frequently with fork to break up clumps. Add the glass of wine. Boil rapidly for about 5 minutes until liquid has reduced slightly. Add the tomatoes, thinly diced and keep tossing until they start melting. Simmer, covered for 45 minutes, stirring occasionally. Meanwhile, in large saucepan, cook the spaghetti according to package directions and drain. Serve sauce immediately over hot spaghetti. Dust with a generous amount of grated Parmesan cheese.

FISH WITH RICE AND VEGETABLES

Ingredients
- 4 teaspoons of parsley, finely chopped
- 2 or 3 hot chilli peppers, finely chopped
- 2 or 3 cloves of minced garlic
- Salt and pepper to taste
- 150-180 grams of white fish in fillets
- 2 tablespoons of olive oil
- 2 onions, chopped
- 300 grams of tomatoes, finely chopped
- 3 carrots, sliced
- 1/4 head of cabbage, cut into wedges
- 1/2 eggplant, cubed
- 60 grams of rice
- Salt and pepper to taste

Preparation Mix the chopped parsley, chilli peppers, garlic, salt and pepper and cover the fillets with it. Heat the oil in a large, deep pot over medium heat. Brown the fish on both

sides in the hot oil and remove to a plate. Add the chopped onions to the hot oil and sauté until cooked through and they are just beginning to brown (about 5 to 7 minutes). Stir in the tomatoes and let them melt, reducing the heat to low. Add some water then add the carrots, cabbage and eggplant and simmer over low heat for 35 minutes, or until the vegetables are cooked but not tender. Add the browned fish and simmer for another 15 minutes or so. Remove the fish and vegetables and about 1 cup of the broth to a platter, cover and set in a warm oven. Strain the remaining broth, discarding the solids. Add enough water to the broth to make 4 cups and return to heat. Bring the broth to a boil, stir in the rice and season with salt and pepper. Reduce heat to medium-low, cover and simmer for 20 minutes, or until the rice is cooked through and tender. Serve the fish over the rice, with vegetables around it.

Variations You can use whole fish or fish fillets. Any firm white-fleshed fish works well. Try this with snails (the best low GI meat you can find). Most vegetables work with this dish: try cassava, potatoes, green beans, zucchini, runner beans or peppers.

CHICKEN NOODLE SOUP

Ingredients
- *1 chicken, whole with skin (best is the corn-fed chicken)*
- *1 onion, roughly chopped*
- *1 celery leg, cut in half*
- *Salt and pepper to taste*
- *1 tablespoon of miso paste*
- *Piece of ginger root*
- *100 grams of rice noodles*
- *1 tablespoon minced garlic*
- *2 teaspoons finely chopped fresh parsley leaves or coriander*
- *1 lime*

Preparation Put the chicken, cut into pieces, the onion and the celery, in a large pan of cold water, add salt and pepper and bring to boil. Let it cook covered for about 1 hour. Then take the chicken out and choose the right amount of stock you need (depends if you are by yourself or feeding others), filter the fat out and put it in a smaller pan. Add the miso paste and two slices of ginger root to the stock and let it boil for 5 minutes. Add the noodles and let them cook for about 4 minutes. Take off the heat and serve in a broth bowl with 90 grams of the skinned chicken meat. Sprinkle with coriander or parsley and a squeeze of lime.

training
programmes

// PLANNING // PREPARING // READY TO RACE

The basics

This section includes training programmes for the 10 km, half-marathon and marathon and there are a wide-range of target times for each so you can find the one most suitable for your running standard and aims. There is also a run-walk programme if you would like to race but find the challenge a bit too daunting initially. This is a great programme to start with as it lets you build-up gradually.

The first thing to be aware of is that there is no one-size-fits-all training programme. The more you train the more you will discover what works for you and what doesn't. For instance, if you find that road running four or five times a week aggravates your muscles and causes injury, then exchange one of your runs on the road for a cross-country run, or you swap an interval session for a spin class in the gym.

Secondly, you should not be a slave to your programme. Although the best results are gained by following a programme to the letter, it is very rare if over the course of the training period you are not ill or pick up niggling injuries. These are signals to pull back and evaluate your options. Be flexible and be prepared to adapt the programme to the situation. To gain the best physiological benefits from your

training you need to be consistent, but running while ill will set your recovery time back and you will simply end up missing further sessions. Also, if you are ill or injured do not try to make up for it by putting in a big training week once you have recovered because you will simply fatigue you body and, again, simply end up missing more in the long term.

Recovery time is vital during a training programme. It is important you get enough sleep ('enough' is different for each person so listen to your body), as well as the correct nutrition and hydration, before, during and after your training sessions. For top athletes, rest and recovery is as vital as the training session itself. For most of us recovery time is difficult to fit in around work, family and social commitments so it is important to be organized and schedule in as much recovery time into your weekly routine as possible.

When choosing a training programme many runners make the mistake of picking a programme that is more advanced than their target goal (eg following a 3 hour 30 mins programme when they are aiming for a 4 hour marathon finish). Although this is done with the best intentions, it means that

the build-up will be too quick and the running volume too great. This means there is a high chance of injury, illness or fatigue, which will lead to de-motivation and a higher possibility of quitting.

Remember that your targets should be challenging but achievable. Have a reason for training. Do you have a specific race in mind (eg New York Marathon) or are you entering a number of endurance events over a season? Whichever it is, it is a good idea to pick your 'A' race as a target, so you can adjust your training programme accordingly. For instance, some runners enter two marathons in the same month but are not sure which is their 'A' race. You should train for the first marathon as if the second wasn't happening, then evaluate how your body feels as you prepare for the second. It's a good idea to plan your 'A' events at the start of the season, as not every race can be a full-out effort.

Before starting a training programme you should have a couple of months with no specific challenges. This is a great time to just go out and simply enjoy running. Leave your heart-rate monitor, stopwatch and GPS running watch behind and just run. Learn to listen to your body, forget

about the usual pressure of set distances and times and just enjoy going out for a run. This is also a good opportunity to find out how to fit running (and recovery) into your weekly routine.

There are four basic types of runs in a programme: long slow distance (LSD), threshold, interval, and easy (or recovery) runs. Programmes also include cross training and/ or stretches and incorporate a taper period at the end to allow your body to recover for your main race. Programmes have a gradual build-up of mileage and intensity, which is vital in the prevention of injury and illness.

Long slow distance runs are all about getting the kilometres under your belt. These runs are the base of all the programmes and without them you will not develop the aerobic base required. However, if you only did this form of training you would never develop the required speed and power. When doing these runs think of 'train don't strain'. You will be building a strong endurance base, teaching your body to utilize its fat stores as an energy source, increasing your Vo2 max and keeping the intensity within its aerobic range. These runs really help you to develop a strong mental toughness.

Threshold runs are all about getting you used to running at pace over an increasing period of time. They are more intense and give your body the ability to recruit more muscle fibres, turn over oxygen quicker, help increase your lactic threshold and improve your running form. The session is designed to make you work hard enough so lactic acid is accumulating in the muscles, but so you can still maintain the pace. This increase of lactate threshold will allow you to sustain a faster pace for your 10 km runs and in the later parts of your half and full marathons when your heart rate will be climbing, even if you are keeping an even pace. There are also psychological benefits for the marathon, as you will be running for a long period above your marathon pace, which gives you added confidence.

Interval sessions are also great at increasing lactic threshold without causing as much damage to your body as the long endurance work. During the high-intensity part of the session your body will be working anaerobically, creating an oxygen debt. During the recovery phase your body will be paying back this oxygen debt, with your heart and lungs combining to do this. In this phase your training zone will drop down to its aerobic phase.

Easy (or recovery) runs are designed to get blood flowing to your legs and aid recovery. They are normally performed after the long run and should help flush out lactic acid which has accumulated from the previous sessions.

At the end of each programme there is a tapering phase. The longer the race the longer the tapering period needs to be. It is vital that you are fresh and carrying no fatigue from any training sessions by the time you get to the starting line. Once you have completed a couple of seasons training and successfully completed in running events, you will find what the best tapering period is for you personally. Always remember that any adaptations from your training take two to three weeks to take effect so there is no point trying to make up for lost time and missed training sessions by training hard a few days before an event.

How to use these programmes

Run-walk programme

The point of this programme is to get over the mental and physical obstacles that are associated with running for a long distance. If you are not used to running this is a great programme to begin with. It starts slowly and gradually builds up so you are getting used to running for a time challenge. Don't worry how much distance you are covering, just keep the walks brisk and the runs as a light jog. If you stick with it your muscles will develop and become stronger to prepare you for the challenges ahead. You will also be surprised how your perspective of running will change; soon a 30-minute run will not seem daunting at all.

How to use

In the run-walk programme the numbers refer to the minutes you should be running and walking respectively and the reps are the number of times you should repeat the cycle that day. So on day 1 of week 1 the programme reads 1 and 3 with x5 reps. This means run for 1 minute, then walk for 3 minutes and repeat the cycle 5 times. Your total training time will be 20 minutes.

Long slow distance runs (LSD)

LSD should be done at around seven to 10 per cent below your target race pace. Going too slowly on LSD can develop poor running form, while going too fast can tire you out for other training sessions. It is important not to push too hard though. Some runners go even slower than the prescribed pace, taking it easy and chatting with friends. LSD is especially important if you are following a marathon training programme which includes a run of up to 35 km (22 miles). If you are following the 5 hour to completion programme for the marathon you should consider incorporating the run-walk strategy into your LSD sessions and running for 5 km (3 miles), then walking briskly for 5 minutes before returning to your run. Repeat the cycle for the rest of your run.

The longest runs in the programme need to be treated with respect. Look at the date for the long runs well in advance and mark the date off in your diary as if it's your mother's birthday – this is not to be missed. If necessary mark the dates where you know you are free and work your way back through the schedule, fitting the rest of the runs around other commitments. Ideally the longest run will be two to three weeks before the event for the marathon, but can be much closer for the shorter distance races. What you don't want is any fatigue left

in the legs from the training runs. The fitter and more used to running your body is, the closer to the event this last long run can be but it is advisable to leave a gap of at least two weeks between your longest training run and the race itself.

Threshold runs

The mid part of this training run should be run at your threshold pace. This pace is where you are unable to sustain a conversation and become breathless quickly. This should be a pace you can sustain from 20 to 60 minutes. If you use a heart rate monitor you will be working around 85 per cent of your maximum heart rate (see Training zones on pages 52-54). For threshold runs you should run the first third of the session warming up to your threshold pace, the middle section sustaining this pace and the final third of the run to ease down off this pace. (eg a 6 km threshold training run = 2 km warming up and gradually increasing pace, 2 km at threshold pace and 2 km easing off pace and warming down.

Intervals (hills at race pace)

Hill training is a great way to build up the strength in your legs (and mind) and is an effective interval training session for your cardio-vascular system. Run at an easy pace for one or two kilometres to

warm up. Then, on a hilly route run at your race pace, aiming to sustain this pace throughout the training session, including up and down the hills. If you are training on steep hills, this will not always be possible and you may have to drop the pace, but try and keep the intensity levels up as you always have the downhill sections to recover.

Intervals (hills)

These sessions can be tough but you should see them as a challenge and not something to fear. As well as building strength and confidence, this part of your training will increase your lactic threshold, allowing you to sustain higher performance levels when it comes to race day. Start with an easy 10 to 15 minute warm-up. Then, on a long, steep hill, run hard uphill for 90 seconds then recover for two to three minutes while jogging downhill back to your starting place. Repeat this by the amount of reps specified in the programme. End your session with an easy 10–minute cool down. You should aim to keep an even pace on each rep and each set (your last hill run should be the same pace as your first), so be careful not to go off too hard. As with most training sessions, the more you practice the more you will learn how to pace the session as a whole.

Intervals (400 metres)

Start with an easy 10 to 15 minute warm-up. Then, using a flat area, run 400 metres at maximum effort followed by a two to three minute light jog to recover. Repeat by the amount of reps listed in the programme. End the session with an easy 10–minute cool down. As with Intervals (hills), the key is to run at an even intensity over each rep and over each set. When many runners first attempt this they go flat out for the first 200 metres, then fail to get anywhere near this pace for the rest of the session. Always make sure you are properly warmed up before attempting the maximum effort. Failure to do this will lead to injury, as you will be working muscle fibres and a range of movement which your body may not have done for a long time (if ever).

Easy (or recovery) runs

Go out for a nice easy jog. These runs are normally after a heavy training day so your legs may feel heavy to start with. Do not worry about the pace and don't push yourself – remember this is a recovery run.

Race pace

Build yourself up to your target race pace, and run at that speed throughout the session. Unlike Intervals (hills at race pace) you should adapt your speed to ensure your intensity levels are even through the run. If you get this right your pace will vary, but the average pace will be at your target race pace.

X-train

Use the cross-training exercises and programmes for strength and core (see Cross training on pages 78-111), focusing on any weaknesses in your body. You can also use this day to do some other type of training such as cycling or swimming. Try not to spend more than an hour working out on your cross-training day.

Rest

No training. Let your body and mind forget about running, and if possible stay off your legs as much as possible. Remember resting means resting so don't be tempted to clean out the attic or spring clean the house. Resting is as important as training hard so on the days where the programme offers a choice between rest and cross training don't always view resting as the soft option.

Stretch

Go to a stretch or yoga class, or spend at least 30 minutes stretching at home or in the gym (see Stretches on pages 69-77).

How to choose your distance and target finish

When deciding what distance to race and at what pace the main thing is to be realistic. There is nothing worse than setting a challenge and having that sense of failure when you realize the task you have chosen is just too far out of your reach.

When setting goals always keep it 'challenging but achievable'. The sense of achievement you will feel on completion of your first marathon, or even first 10 km, is a great feeling you will want to repeat again and again. It is the type of feeling that will keep you pushing for greater goals. Some people cannot even contemplate running for 10 minutes without stopping and yet with the proper training they can go on to finish a marathon. Even if this journey takes years it doesn't matter because there is a lot of enjoyment along the way as well as the associated health benefits, weight loss and so on.

Choosing the right target time is especially important with the longer distances. Many runners pluck times out of the air, start the training schedules and find the distance and time commitment are simply too arduous. Remember: the reason finishing a marathon

is such an achievement is because it is tough and training is a big commitment. The average marathon finishing time is around 4 hours 30 minutes for men and 5 hours 10 minutes for women. This, of course, varies depending on the course and the weather conditions.

So how do you choose what distance to aim for and which training programme to use? The race time prediction chart below provides a useful guideline for predicting your 10 km, half-marathon, and marathon target time once you have a 5 km time to work from. Simply find your 5 km time on the left of the chart and read across to see your predicted time for longer distances

Race time prediction chart

5 km Mins	10 km Mins	21.1 km Hours	42.2 km Hours
17.30	36.00	1.20	2.51
20.00	42.00	1.32	3.15
22.30	47.00	1.43	3.39
25.00	52.00	1.55	4.05
27.30	57.00	2.07	4.29
30.00	63.00	2.17	4.52
32.30	68.00	2.29	5.17
35.00	73.00	2.41	5.41
37.30	78.00	2.52	6.06
40.00	83.00	3.04	6.30

But be aware that these are only guidelines to start your training. Bodies are built differently and we all have different running skills. Some people can run a fast 5 km but find they slow down dramatically when they race a half-marathon whereas other runners seem able to sustain their 10 km pace over the half-marathon distance. Be prepared to adjust your goals as you get into your training programme.

Finding your target time

1. If you can't run for more than 30 minutes then start with the run-walk programme (see page 154). This will give you a very gradual build-up and a solid base.

2. Once you can run for more than 30 minutes continuously then move onto the 10 km under 60 mins programme (see page 154). This is a short programme and you will soon find yourself running faster.

3. Once you feel ready, mark out a flat 5 km course and time yourself. Now you have your 5 km time you can use the prediction chart to predict your time for longer distances and choose your programme accordingly.

Run-walk

Training programme for run-walk for base training

	Reps	Day 1	Day 2	Day 3	Day 4	Day 5	Day 6	Day 7
Week 1	x5	1 and 3	Core	1 and 3	Rest or X-train	1 and 3	Stretch	Rest
Week 2	x6	2 and 2	Core	2 and 2	Rest or X-train	2 and 2	Stretch	Rest
Week 3	x5	3 and 2	Core	3 and 2	Rest or X-train	3 and 2	Stretch	Rest
Week 4	x5	3 and 1	Core	3 and 1	Rest or X-train	3 and 1	Stretch	Rest
Week 5	x5	4 and 1	Core	4 and 1	Rest or X-train	4 and 1	Stretch	Rest
Week 6	x4	6 and 1	Core	8 and 1	Rest or X-train	6 and 1	Stretch	Rest
Week 7	x4	8 and 1	Core	7 and 1	Rest or X-train	9 and 1	Stretch	Rest
Week 8	x4	10 and 1	Core	10 and 1	Rest or X-train	10 and 1	Stretch	Rest
Week 9	x5	10 and 1	Core	10 and 1	Rest or X-train	Run 40 (x1 rep)	Stretch	Rest
Week 10	x1	Run 45	Core	Run 10	Rest	Run 50	Stretch	Rest

10 km

Training programme for 10 km in under 60 mins

	Day 1	Day 2	Day 3	Day 4	Day 5	Day 6	Day 7
	Easy	Threshold	Rest or X-train	Intervals (400 metres)	Stretch	Rest	LSD
Week 1	3 km	3 km	Rest or X-train	3 reps x 400 m	Stretch	Rest	3 km
Week 2	5 km	5 km	Rest or X-train	3 reps x 400 m	Stretch	Rest	5 km
Week 3	5 km	5 km	Rest or X-train	4 reps x 400 m	Stretch	Rest	7 km
Week 4	5 km	5 km	Rest or X-train	4 reps x 400 m	Stretch	Rest	9 km
Week 5	5 km	7 km	Rest or X-train	4 reps x 400 m	Stretch	Rest	10 km
Week 6	5 km	7 km	Rest or X-train	4 reps x 400 m	Stretch	Rest	8 km
Week 7	5 km	7 km	Rest or X-train	5 reps x 400 m	Stretch	Rest	10 km
Week 8	3 km	7 km	Rest	3 reps x 400 m	Stretch	Rest	Race

Training programme for 10 km in under 55 mins

	Day 1	Day 2	Day 3	Day 4	Day 5	Day 6	Day 7
	Easy	Threshold	Rest or X-train	Intervals (400 metres)	Stretch	Rest	LSD
Week 1	3 km	3 km	Rest or X-train	3 reps x 400 m	Stretch	Rest	3 km
Week 2	5 km	5 km	Rest or X-train	3 reps x 400 m	Stretch	Rest	5 km
Week 3	5 km	5 km	Rest or X-train	4 reps x 400 m	Stretch	Rest	7 km
Week 4	5 km	6 km	Rest or X-train	4 reps x 400 m	Stretch	Rest	9 km
Week 5	5 km	6 km	Rest or X-train	5 reps x 400 m	Stretch	Rest	10 km
Week 6	5 km	7 km	Rest or X-train	5 reps x 400 m	Stretch	Rest	11 km
Week 7	5 km	8 km	Rest or X-train	6 reps x 400 m	Stretch	Rest	10 km
Week 8	3 km	5 km	Rest	3 reps x 400 m	Stretch	Rest	Race

Training programme for 10 km in under 50 mins

	Day 1	Day 2	Day 3	Day 4	Day 5	Day 6	Day 7
	Easy	Threshold	Rest or X-train	Intervals (400 metres)	Stretch	Rest	LSD
Week 1	3 km	3 km	Rest or X-train	3 reps x 400 m	Stretch	Rest	3 km
Week 2	5 km	5 km	Rest or X-train	4 reps x 400 m	Stretch	Rest	5 km
Week 3	5 km	5 km	Rest or X-train	4 reps x 400 m	Stretch	Rest	7 km
Week 4	5 km	7 km	Rest or X-train	5 reps x 400 m	Stretch	Rest	9 km
Week 5	5 km	7 km	Rest or X-train	5 reps x 400 m	Stretch	Rest	12 km
Week 6	5 km	8 km	Rest or X-train	6 reps x 400 m	Stretch	Rest	10 km
Week 7	5 km	8 km	Rest or X-train	6 reps x 400 m	Stretch	Rest	10 km
Week 8	5 km	6 km	Rest or X-train	4 reps x 400 m	Stretch	Rest	Race

Training programme for 10 km in under 45 mins

	Day 1	Day 2	Day 3	Day 4	Day 5	Day 6	Day 7
	Easy	Threshold	Rest or X-train	Intervals (400 metres)	Interval (hills)	Rest	LSD
Week 1	3 km	3 km	Rest or X-train	3 reps x 400 m	3 km	Rest	4 km
Week 2	5 km	5 km	Rest or X-train	4 reps x 400 m	4 km	Rest	6 km
Week 3	5 km	6 km	Rest or X-train	4 reps x 400 m	5 km	Rest	9 km
Week 4	5 km	7 km	Rest or X-train	5 reps x 400 m	5 km	Rest	12 km
Week 5	5 km	8 km	Rest or X-train	5 reps x 400 m	5 km	Rest	14 km
Week 6	5 km	8 km	Rest or X-train	6 reps x 400 m	6 km	Rest	12 km
Week 7	5 km	8 km	Rest or X-train	6 reps x 400 m	7 km	Rest	10 km
Week 8	5 km	7 km	Rest	4 reps x 400 m	4 km	Rest	Race

Half-marathon

Training programme for a half-marathon in under 2 hours 15 mins

	Day 1	Day 2	Day 3	Day 4	Day 5	Day 6	Day 7
	Easy	Rest or X-train	Threshold	Rest	Intervals (hills race pace)	Stretch	LSD
Week 1	3 km	Rest or X-train	3 km	Rest	3 km	Stretch	5 km
Week 2	3 km	Rest or X-train	5 km	Rest	3 km	Stretch	5 km
Week 3	3 km	Rest or X-train	6 km	Rest	5 km	Stretch	6 km
Week 4	5 km	Rest or X-train	6 km	Rest	5 km	Stretch	8 km
Week 5	5 km	Rest or X-train	8 km	Rest	3 km	Stretch	11 km
Week 6	5 km	Rest or X-train	5 km	Rest	5 km	Stretch	10 km timed
Week 7	5 km	Rest or X-train	8 km	Rest	6 km	Stretch	8 km
Week 8	5 km	Rest or X-train	8 km	Rest	8 km	Stretch	11 km
Week 9	5 km	Rest or X-train	8 km	Rest	6 km	Stretch	14 km
Week 10	5 km	Rest or X-train	8 km	Rest	6 km	Stretch	18 km
Week 11	5 km	Rest or X-train	8 km	Rest	6 km	Stretch	10 km
Week 12	5 km	Rest	5 km	Rest	3 km	Stretch	Race

Training programme for a half-marathon in under 2 hours

	Day 1	Day 2	Day 3	Day 4	Day 5	Day 6	Day 7
	Easy	Rest or X-train	Threshold	Rest	Intervals (hills race pace)	Stretch	LSD
Week 1	3 km	Rest or X-train	5 km	Rest	3 km	Stretch	6 km
Week 2	5 km	Rest or X-train	5 km	Rest	3 km	Stretch	6 km
Week 3	8 km	Rest or X-train	6 km	Rest	5 km	Stretch	8 km
Week 4	8 km	Rest or X-train	6 km	Rest	5 km	Stretch	10 km
Week 5	8 km	Rest or X-train	8 km	Rest	6 km	Stretch	13 km
Week 6	8 km	Rest or X-train	5 km	Rest	5 km	Stretch	10 km race
Week 7	8 km	Rest or X-train	8 km	Rest	6 km	Stretch	11 km
Week 8	8 km	Rest or X-train	10 km	Rest	8 km	Stretch	13 km
Week 9	8 km	Rest or X-train	10 km	Rest	8 km	Stretch	16 km
Week 10	8 km	Rest or X-train	8 km	Rest	8 km	Stretch	18 km
Week 11	8 km	Rest or X-train	8 km	Rest	10 km	Stretch	10 km
Week 12	8 km	Rest	5 km	Rest	3 km	Stretch	Race

Training programme for a half-marathon in under sub 1 hour 45 mins

	Day 1	Day 2	Day 3	Day 4	Day 5	Day 6	Day 7
	Easy	Rest or X-train	Threshold	Race pace	Intervals (hills race pace)	Rest or stretch	LSD
Week 1	5 km	Rest or X-train	5 km	5 km	5 km	Rest	6 km
Week 2	6 km	Rest or X-train	5 km	5 km	8 km	Rest	10 km
Week 3	6 km	Rest or X-train	6 km	5 km	8 km	Rest	11 km
Week 4	8 km	Rest or X-train	6 km	6 km	8 km	Rest	13 km
Week 5	8 km	Rest or X-train	8 km	6 km	5 km	Rest	13 km
Week 6	8 km	Rest or X-train	8 km	6 km	8 km	Rest	10 km race
Week 7	8 km	Rest or X-train	10 km	8 km	10 km	Rest	13 km
Week 8	8 km	Rest or X-train	11 km	8 km	10 km	Rest	16 km
Week 9	8 km	Rest or X-train	11 km	8 km	10 km	Rest	19 km
Week 10	8 km	Rest or X-train	13 km	8 km	10 km	Rest	23 km
Week 11	6 km	Rest or X-train	10 km	8 km	10 km	Rest	13 km
Week 12	6 km	Rest	3 km easy	3 km easy	5 km easy	Rest	Race

Training programme for a half-marathon in under sub 1 hour 35 mins

	Day 1	Day 2	Day 3	Day 4	Day 5	Day 6	Day 7
	Easy	Rest or X-train	Threshold	Race pace	Intervals (hills race pace)	Rest or stretch	LSD
Week 1	5 km	Rest or X-train	5 km	5 km	5 km	Rest	10 km
Week 2	6 km	Rest or X-train	6 km	6 km	6 km	Rest	13 km
Week 3	8 km	Rest or X-train	8 km	8 km	6 km	Rest	13 km
Week 4	8 km	Rest or X-train	10 km	8 km	8 km	Rest	16 km
Week 5	8 km	Rest or X-train	10 km	8 km	10 km	Rest	16 km
Week 6	8 km	Rest or X-train	11 km	8 km	10 km	Rest	19 km
Week 7	8 km	Rest or X-train	11 km	8 km	6 km	Rest	10 km race
Week 8	8 km	Rest or X-train	13 km	8 km	10 km	Rest	23 km
Week 9	8 km	Rest or X-train	13 km	8 km	10 km	Rest	24 km
Week 10	8 km	Rest or X-train	14 km	8 km	11 km	Rest	19 km
Week 11	8 km	Rest or X-train	16 km	8 km	11 km	Rest	13 km
Week 12	8 km	Rest	6 km	5 km	3 km	Rest	Race

Marathon

Training programme for a marathon in 5 hours to completion

	Day 1 Easy	Day 2 Rest or X-train	Day 3 Threshold	Day 4 Rest	Day 5 Intervals (hills race pace)	Day 6 Rest and stretch	Day 7 LSD
Week 1	5 km	Rest or X-train	6 km	Rest	3 km	Rest	6 km
Week 2	5 km	Rest or X-train	6 km	Rest	3 km	Rest	10 km
Week 3	5 km	Rest or X-train	8 km	Rest	5 km	Rest	13 km
Week 4	6 km	Rest or X-train	8 km	Rest	5 km	Rest	13 km
Week 5	6 km	Rest or X-train	10 km	Rest	3 km	Rest	16 km
Week 6	8 km	Rest or X-train	10 km	Rest	5 km	Rest	19 km
Week 7	8 km	Rest or X-train	6 km	Rest	3 km	Rest	21.1 km race
Week 8	8 km	Rest or X-train	6 km	Rest	5 km	Rest	26 km
Week 9	8 km	Rest or X-train	13 km	Rest	6 km	Rest	19 km
Week 10	8 km	Rest or X-train	8 km	Rest	3 km	Rest	29 km
Week 11	8 km	Rest or X-train	16 km	Rest	8 km	Rest	16 km
Week 12	8 km	Rest or X-train	6 km	Rest	3 km	Rest	32 km
Week 13	8 km	Rest or X-train	8 km	Rest	8 km	Rest	24 km
Week 14	8 km	Rest or X-train	8 km	Rest	6 km	Rest	16 km
Week 15	8 km	Rest or X-train	3 km easy	Rest	3 km easy	Rest	10 km
Week 16	5 km	Rest	2 km easy	Rest	2 km easy	Rest	Race

Training programme for a marathon in under 4 hours 30 mins

	Day 1 Easy	Day 2 Rest or X-train	Day 3 Threshold	Day 4 Race pace or rest	Day 5 Intervals (hills race pace)	Day 6 Rest and stretch	Day 7 LSD
Week 1	5 km	Rest or X-train	5 km	5 km	5 km	Rest	10 km
Week 2	6 km	Rest or X-train	6 km	6 km	5 km	Rest	11 km
Week 3	8 km	Rest or X-train	6 km	8 km	6 km	Rest	13 km
Week 4	8 km	Rest or X-train	8 km	8 km	6 km	Rest	16 km
Week 5	8 km	Rest or X-train	8 km	8 km	6 km	Rest	16 km
Week 6	8 km	Rest or X-train	10 km	8 km	6 km	Rest	19 km
Week 7	8 km	Rest or X-train	10 km	8 km	6 km	Rest	19 km
Week 8	8 km	Rest or X-train	11 km	8 km	6 km	Rest	21.1 km race
Week 9	8 km	Rest or X-train	8 km	8 km	6 km	Rest	26 km
Week 10	8 km	Rest or X-train	8 km	8 km	6 km	Rest	23 km
Week 11	8 km	Rest or X-train	13 km	8 km	8 km	Rest	24 km
Week 12	8 km	Rest or X-train	14 km	8 km	6 km	Rest	29 km
Week 13	8 km	Rest or X-train	16 km	8 km	8 km	Rest	26 km
Week 14	8 km	Rest or X-train	8 km	8 km	5 km	Rest	32 km
Week 15	8 km	Rest or X-train	5 km	5 km	5 km	Rest	16 km
Week 16	5 km	Rest	3 km easy	Rest	3 km easy	Rest	Race

Training programme a marathon in under 4 hours

	Day 1	Day 2	Day 3	Day 4	Day 5	Day 6	Day 7
	Easy	Rest or X-train	Threshold	Race pace or rest	Intervals (hills race pace)	Rest and stretch	LSD
Week 1	5 km	Rest or X-train	5 km	5 km	5 km	Rest	8 km
Week 2	6 km	Rest or X-train	6 km	6 km	5 km	Rest	13 km
Week 3	8 km	Rest or X-train	6 km	8 km	6 km	Rest	13 km
Week 4	8 km	Rest or X-train	8 km	8 km	6 km	Rest	16 km
Week 5	8 km	Rest or X-train	8 km	8 km	8 km	Rest	16 km
Week 6	8 km	Rest or X-train	10 km	8 km	8 km	Rest	19 km
Week 7	8 km	Rest or X-train	10 km	8 km	10 km	Rest	19 km
Week 8	8 km	Rest or X-train	11 km	8 km	10 km	Rest	23 km/21.1 race
Week 9	8 km	Rest or X-train	8 km	8 km	6 km	Rest	26 km
Week 10	8 km	Rest or X-train	8 km	8 km	6 km	Rest	29 km
Week 11	8 km	Rest or X-train	13 km	8 km	10 km	Rest	23 km
Week 12	8 km	Rest or X-train	14 km	8 km	6 km	Rest	29 km
Week 13	8 km	Rest or X-train	16 km	8 km	10 km	Rest	26 km
Week 14	8 km	Rest or X-train	8 km	8 km	5 km	Rest	32 km
Week 15	8 km	Rest or X-train	5 km	5 km	5 km	Rest	16 km
Week 16	5 km	Rest	3 km easy	Rest	3 km easy	Rest	Race

Training programme a marathon in under 3 hours 30 mins

	Day 1	Day 2	Day 3	Day 4	Day 5	Day 6	Day 7
	Easy	Threshold or X-train	Race pace	Race pace (hills)	Intervals and stretch	Rest	LSD
Week 1	8 km	8 km	5 km	8 km	3 reps	Rest	13 km
Week 2	8 km	11 km	8 km	8 km	4 reps	Rest	16 km
Week 3	8 km	14 km	8 km	8 km	4 reps	Rest	19 km
Week 4	8 km	14 km	8 km	11 km	5 reps	Rest	23 km
Week 5	8 km	16 km	8 km	11 km	5 reps	Rest	16 km
Week 6	8 km	16 km	8 km	14 km	6 reps	Rest	26 km
Week 7	8 km	19 km	8 km	14 km	6 reps	Rest	19 km
Week 8	8 km	19 km	8 km	16 km	7 reps	Rest	29 km
Week 9	8 km	23 km	8 km	8 km	8 reps	Rest	21.1 km race
Week 10	8 km	23 km	8 km	16 km	5 km easy	Rest	32 km
Week 11	8 km	19 km	8 km	13 km	8 reps	Rest	26 km
Week 12	8 km	16 km	8 km	16 km	5 easy	Rest	29 km
Week 13	8 km	26 km	8 km	16 km	8 reps	Rest	26 km
Week 14	8 km	16 km	8 km	8 km	8 km easy	Rest	32-35 km
Week 15	8 km	6 km	5 km	3 km easy	3 km easy	Rest	16 km
Week 16	5 km	3 km easy	Rest	3 km easy	Rest	Rest	Race

First published in 2011 by
New Holland Publishers (UK) Ltd
London • Cape Town • Sydney • Auckland
www.newhollandpublishers.com

Garfield House	80 McKenzie	Unit 1, 66	218 Lake Road
86–88 Edgware	Street	Gibbes Street,	Northcote
Road	Cape Town 8001	Chatswood	Auckland
London W2 2EA	South Africa	NSW 2067	New Zealand
United Kingdom		Australia	

Copyright © 2011 New Holland Publishers (UK) Ltd
Copyright © 2011 in text: Daniel Ford

The authors have asserted their morals rights to be identified as the authors of this work.

All rights reserved. No part of this publication may be reproduced, stored in a retrieval system or transmitted, in any form or by any means, electronic, mechanical, photocopying, recording or otherwise, without the prior written permission of the publishers and copyright holders.

A catalogue record for this book is available from the British Library.

ISBN 978 1 84773 875 2

This book has been produced for New Holland Publishers by
Chase My Snail Ltd
www.chasemysnail.com
London • Cape Town

Project Manager: Daniel Ford
Designer: Darren Exell
Photo Editor: Anthony Ernest
Publisher: Guy Hobbs
Production: Marion Storz
Illustrators: Juliet Percival and James Berrangé

2 4 6 8 10 9 7 5 3 1

Reproduction by Pica Digital Pte Ltd, Singapore
Printed and bound in Singapore by Craft Print International Ltd.

The authors and publishers have made every effort to ensure that all information given in this book is accurate, but they cannot accept liability for any resulting injury or loss or damage to either property or person, whether direct or consequential and howsoever arising.